Africa Society of Evangelical Theology Series

We often hear these days that the center of Christianity is moving toward the Global South and Africa is a key player in that movement. This makes the study of African Christianity and African realities important – even more so when it is being done by Africans themselves and in their own context. The Africa Society of Evangelical Theology (ASET) was created to encourage research and sustained theological reflection on key issues facing Africa by and for African Christians and those working within African contexts. The volumes in this series constitute the best papers presented at the annual conferences of ASET and together they seek to fill this important gap in the literature of Christianity.

Titles in This Series

Christianity and Suffering: African Perspectives
2017 | 9781783683604

African Contextual Realities
2018 | 9781783684731

Governance and Christian Higher Education in the African Context
2019 | 9781783685455

God and Creation
2019 | 9781783687565

Forgiveness, Peacemaking, and Reconciliation
2020 | 9781839730535

Who Do You Say I Am? Christology in Africa
2021 | 9781839735325

For more information about the Africa Society of Evangelical Theology,
see the Society's Facebook page at:
https://www.facebook.com/AfricaSocietyOfEvangelicalTheology/
or contact ASET at: asetsecretary@gmail.com

In some Christian circles the Holy Spirit is associated primarily with extraordinary phenomena. In others, one might feel like the disciples in Ephesus who told Paul, "We have not even heard that there is a Holy Spirit." This edited volume offers a valuable overview of African conversations for Westerners like me, while continuing those conversations with humility, diversity and probing discernment. This book offers a great model. Talking together about the Holy Spirit, while displaying the fruit of the Spirit, this book offers not only great insight but a terrific model for how that is done.

Michael Horton, PhD
J. Gresham Machen Professor of Theology,
Westminster Seminary California, USA

Infused with astute research and scholarship, this collection of essays exposes the perspective shifts, conflicting doctrines and misunderstood realities about the role and identity of the Holy Spirit in building the called-out community of God in Africa. The volume unpacks the African concept of Christian community and the role of the Holy Spirit in building that community with insights from the Pentecost event to our post-modern era. This book is not only one for theologians but provides insights for the many who are interested in deepening the holistic impact of their congregations on society through the works of the Holy Spirit.

John K. Jusu, PhD
Africa International University, Kenya
Regional Director for Anglophone Africa,
United World Mission/Overseas Council

ASET
SERIES

The Holy Spirit in African Christianity

GLOBAL LIBRARY

The Holy Spirit in African Christianity

General Editors

David K. Ngaruiya
and
Rodney L. Reed

GLOBAL LIBRARY

© 2022 Africa Society of Evangelical Theology (ASET)

Published 2022 by Langham Global Library
An imprint of Langham Publishing
www.langhampublishing.org

Langham Publishing and its imprints are a ministry of Langham Partnership

Langham Partnership
PO Box 296, Carlisle, Cumbria, CA3 9WZ, UK
www.langham.org

ISBNs:
978-1-83973-646-9 Print
978-1-83973-743-5 ePub
978-1-83973-744-2 Mobi
978-1-83973-745-9 PDF

David K. Ngariuya and Rodney L. Reed hereby assert their moral right to be identified as the Author of the General Editor's part in the Work in accordance with sections 77 and 78 of the Copyright, Designs and Patents Act 1988.

All rights reserved. No part of this publication may be reproduced, stored in a retrieval system or transmitted, in any form or by any means, electronic, mechanical, photocopying, recording or otherwise, without the prior written permission of the publisher or the Copyright Licensing Agency.

Requests to reuse content from Langham Publishing are processed through PLSclear. Please visit www.plsclear.com to complete your request.

All Scripture quotations, unless otherwise indicated, are taken from the Holy Bible, New International Version®, NIV®. Copyright ©1973, 1978, 1984, 2011 by Biblica, Inc.™ Used by permission of Zondervan.

Scripture quotations marked NASB are taken from the New American Standard Bible®, Copyright © 1960, 1962, 1963, 1968, 1971, 1972, 1973, 1975, 1977, 1995 by The Lockman Foundation. Used by permission.

Scripture quotations marked ESV are from The Holy Bible, English Standard Version® (ESV®), copyright © 2001 by Crossway, a publishing ministry of Good News Publishers. Used by permission. All rights reserved.

Scripture quotations marked NRSV are from the New Revised Standard Version Bible, copyright © 1989 National Council of the Churches of Christ in the United States of America. Used by permission. All rights reserved.

British Library Cataloguing-in-Publication Data
A catalogue record for this book is available from the British Library

ISBN: 978-1-83973-646-9

Cover & Book Design: projectluz.com

Langham Partnership actively supports theological dialogue and an author's right to publish but does not necessarily endorse the views and opinions set forth here or in works referenced within this publication, nor can we guarantee technical and grammatical correctness. Langham Partnership does not accept any responsibility or liability to persons or property as a consequence of the reading, use or interpretation of its published content.

Contents

Preface xi

Acknowledgments xiii

1 An Inclusive Rereading of Acts 2:1–47 for Enhancing Partnership in Ministry. 1
   Moses Iliya Ogidis

2 A Comparison of the Montanists and the Pentecostals in Their Expression of the Reception of the Holy Spirit in Christian History . 17
   Kwaku Boamah and Jacob Kwame Opata

3 Augustine's Articulation of the Holy Spirit. 33
   David K. Ngaruiya

4 Pneumatology and Mission of the Church in Postmodern Africa . . . 49
   The Holy Spirit in Trinitarian Theology as Panacea
   John Michael Kiboi

5 In Dialogue with the Jehovah's Witnesses. 71
   The "Name" of the Holy Spirit
   Jeffrey S. Krohn

6 "I Banged the Table Three Times" 91
   The Empowering Spirit and Women in the AINC
   Esther Mombo and Heleen Joziasse

7 The Comparative Study of the Work of the Holy Spirit in African Independent Churches and African Pentecostal Churches in Botswana 105
   Kenosi Molato

8 Perceptions of the Holy Spirit's Deliverance in Ghanaian Charismatic Ministries 125
   Assessing the Work of J. Kwabena Asamoah-Gyadu
   Stephanie A. Lowery and Danson Ottawa Wafula

List of Contributors 143

Subject Index. 147

Scripture Index 151

Preface

Doctrine unites, doctrine divides and doctrine reflects the rich diversity of Christian heritage and particularly so on issues related to the Holy Spirit. In African Christianity, the understanding and practices related to the Holy Spirit come in varied shades of a multicolored theological garment. In charismatic churches, the Holy Spirit working is emphasized in bold and flamboyant shades. Mainstream churches in this regard also emphasize the work of the Holy Spirit but with more subdued shades though with regular confession that includes the Holy Spirit. Among various African indigenous churches, the Holy Spirit receives much emphasis in colors that stretch the entire spectrum. Nevertheless, regardless of denominational, cultural or theological heritage, virtually all African Christians include the Holy Spirit in their regular confessions.

The church of Jesus Christ has, over the centuries, been plagued by misunderstandings and controversies regarding the Holy Spirit. In some situations, the Holy Spirit has been used to mask the work of false prophets who as Christ pointed out "perform miracles," "drive out demons" and "prophesy" (Matt 7:22). Rather than be deified in reference as a fully divine person, the Holy Spirit is often objectified as a force that is impersonal, inanimate and vague. In its rise, Pentecostalism has also ignited an ongoing debate regarding infilling of the Holy Spirit, his indwelling and his baptism. Thus, it is critical that this volume on the Holy Spirit in African Christianity addresses some of these issues among many other concerns.

The importance of the Holy Spirit in God's economy is without doubt among Christian Africans. The challenge in African Christianity in this matter is the documentation on ways the Holy Spirit is understood. Taking into account that Africans were witnesses to the outpouring of the Holy Spirit at Pentecost, there ought to be rich available literature on this matter, but this is not the case at the present moment. Derived from the 2021 Africa Society of Evangelical Theology (ASET) conference, hosted virtually by the International Leadership University, this seventh volume of the Africa Society of Evangelical series seeks to begin to address that notable gap. Some may contend while others concur that theology should consider starting contouring itself commencing with the Holy Spirit; this in itself is a recognition that the Holy Spirit is sometimes relegated to the fringes in the development of Christian doctrine.

The volume features an array of essays on the Holy Spirit in African Christianity. The first three essays feature a rereading of Acts 2:1–47, comparing how the Montanists and Pentecostals express themselves in regard to the Holy Spirit and articulation of the Holy Spirit by Augustine. This is followed by an exploration of the Holy Spirit and church's mission in postmodern Africa, the contention of the Jehovah Witnesses that the Holy Spirit has no name and the Holy Spirit's empowerment and women in African Instituted Churches. The last essays focus on comparing the work of the Holy Spirit in African Independent Churches and African Pentecostal churches and perceptions of the Spirit's work in deliverance.

David K. Ngaruiya, PhD

Acknowledgments

The chapters that follow represent the best of papers presented at the eleventh annual conference of the Africa Society of Evangelical Theology (ASET), which took place at International Leadership University (ILU) in Nairobi, Kenya on 5–6 March 2021. This conference took place in the midst of the COVID-19 pandemic which changed our world. As a testimony to that, this was the first ASET conference held virtually. Despite the negative effect of the pandemic, this volume contains a strong international flavor, with contributions from scholars either originally from or now serving in Kenya, Ethiopia, the United States, the Netherlands, Botswana, Nigeria, Zimbabwe and Ghana. That, we discern, is one of the positive serendipities of having a virtual conference.

The Editorial Committee of ASET wishes to thank the host of the conference at which these papers were presented, International Leadership University. ILU demonstrated its flexibility by enabling the conference to go "virtual." We thank the contributors of these papers who patiently worked with the Editorial Committee to make several revisions. We acknowledge the important role of our reviewers, both of the conference proposals and post-conference papers, as well as Prof. Nathan Chiroma for his input to the volume index. Their work was essential in identifying the "cream of the crop" and making that cream taste even better. We also owe a great debt of gratitude to the team at Langham Publishing. Langham has walked this journey with ASET now to its seventh volume. Finally to my editorial partner, David Ngaruiya, thank you so much for helping to shoulder the load. "Two are better than one, because they have a good return for their labor" (Eccl 4:9).

Rodney L. Reed, PhD

1

An Inclusive Rereading of Acts 2:1–47 for Enhancing Partnership in Ministry

Moses Iliya Ogidis
Serving with Evangelical Church Winning All in Nigeria and PhD Candidate, St. Paul's University, Limuru, Kenya

Abstract

The book of Acts describes the growth of the early church. The coming down of the Holy Spirit on the day of Pentecost is a notable event in the life of the early believers. The Holy Spirit came on the followers of Christ and empowered them for the ministry of spreading the gospel. Even though – after the coming down of the Holy Spirit – the early church faced challenges like persecution, they remained firm due to dependence on the Holy Spirit. The outpouring of the Holy Spirit on the believers as recorded in Acts 2:1–47, was not discriminatory. The impact of their dependence on the Holy Spirit is evident in the quality of ministry at that time. The early church as shown in Acts 2:1–47 is renowned for standing out in inclusive ministry, particularly in the household churches where both men and women played various leadership roles. Besides, the early believers (the church) are famed for their distinctive fellowship rooted in love, unity and constant prayers for one another. It is from this backdrop that a reading of Acts 2:1–47 is considered as a model for the contemporary evangelical churches in Nigeria toward a spirit-driven partnership between men, women, young people and people with disabilities in ministry. This paper holds that exclusive dependence on the Holy Spirit, as exemplified by the early church, will result in a thriving Spirit-driven partnership of women and men, the young and the old and people living with disabilities in spreading the gospel and in ordained ministry. This is because the Holy Spirit bonds all people in a common vision of enhancing the kingdom of God in prayer, fellowship, teaching, sharing with those in need and reaching out to others while awaiting the second coming of our Lord and Savior Jesus Christ.

Key words: Inclusivity, Holy Spirit, Acts 2, Pentecost, Nigerian Church, Ministry

Introduction

The book of Acts describes the growth and expansion of the church, which is built on the promise of Jesus Christ to his followers, whom he told to go and wait for the Holy Spirit in Jerusalem (Acts 1:8). John Stott observes that "throughout Luke's narratives there are references to the promise, gift, outpouring, baptism, fullness, power, witness and guidance of the Holy Spirit. It is impossible to explain the progress of the gospel apart from the work of the Spirit."[1] It is imperative that the book can be referred to as "the book of the Holy Spirit" or "the book on the works of the Holy Spirit" starting from the beginning of the church to the end of the age. The Holy Spirit came upon the followers of Jesus as evidenced in the book of Acts, and as Jesus promised in John 14:15–17, to teach and comfort his followers, among other things.

The coming of the Holy Spirit in Acts 2 brought the fulfillment of what had been predicted in the Old Testament (in Joel) and echoed by Jesus in John's Gospel. The promised Holy Spirit is to come on all human beings; young and old, male and female, irrespective of nationality, race and ethnic group. Nevertheless, there are challenges when it comes to the role of people in the ministry of the "Word of God" (ordination). Some are discriminated based on their gender, race, ethnicity, age and even nationality. These have been the challenges in most of the evangelical churches in Nigeria when it comes to including women, young people and those with disabilities as partners in the ministry (as ordained ministers). The discrimination of other people (women, young people and people with disabilities) when it comes to their inclusion into the ministry of the Word appears to be contrary to what happened in Acts 2. This resonates with what Mercy Oduyoye argues that whatever is keeping

---

1. Stott, *Message of Acts*, 33.

the subordination of women, young people, those with disabilities, racism and tribalism alive in the church cannot be the Spirit of God.[2]

Therefore, this paper aims at a rereading that is all-inclusive of people with disabilities,[3] gender, nationality, tribes, races and ethnicity, among others. The outpouring of the Holy Spirit in Acts 2 is not discriminating, selecting or hierarchical and does not oppress or subordinate people. This article is divided into the following sections: the background of the church in Acts, the church in Nigeria (evangelicals) and the inclusive reading for mutual partnership in ministry for all. This paper considers the evangelical churches such as Evangelical Church Winning All (ECWA), Evangelical Reform Church of Christ (ERCC), Church of Christ in Nations (COCIN) among others that have not yet accepted the inclusion of women into the ministry of the word of God (ordination).

Background to the Book of Acts

The book of Acts records the early history of the church immediately after the ascension of Jesus Christ to heaven. In regard to its authorship, David Williams asserts that "it is almost an axiom of the New Testament scholarship that whoever wrote the third Gospel was also the author of Acts. Traditionally, he has been identified with Luke, Paul's companion and physician."[4] The early church fathers since Irenaeus and the Muratorian canon also attributed the authorship to Luke, the companion of Paul.[5] Other scholars such as John Stott, Carl Holladay and Martin Dibelius argued that the form and content of both the Gospel of Luke and Acts work as a single, two-volume work. The similarity of language and style and the theological purpose of both books leaves no doubt that the two are from the same source and author. There are no serious doubts on the authorship of the book; the majority of scholars and commentators accepts that Luke wrote it together with the gospel.

---

2. Oduyoye, *Daughters of Anowa*, 182.

3. This paper will use the phrase "people with disabilities" for those with visual, physical, speaking, hearing impairments, not all the forms of disabilities. Impairment is a problem in body function or structure; an activity limitation is a difficulty encountered by an individual in executing a task or action; while a participation restriction is a problem experienced by an individual in involvement in life situations. See Towards a Common Language for Functioning, Disability and Health ICF. World Health Organization Geneva 2002. https://cdn.who.int/media/docs/default-source/classification/icf/icfbeginnersguide.pdf.

4. Williams, *Acts*, 2.

5. Dibelius, *Book of Acts*, 3, and see also Holladay, *Acts*, 2–4.

The book of Acts is believed to have several purposes. The main reason Luke wrote the book of Acts can be seen in Acts 1:1–2 where his concern was to trace the continuation of the ministry Jesus Christ started by the disciples and the beginning of the Christian church. It was written to show how the new movement within the Roman Empire was successful through the power of the Holy Spirit, which led to the Gentile mission through the commissioning of Paul (Saul) in Acts 9. Furthermore, Richard Longenecker avers that its composition is also *kerygmatic* (which means "preaching" or "proclamation"). It shows how the gospel is related to the course of redemptive history (all human beings), and how gospel preaching is having the power of the Holy Spirit backing every believer that proclaims it (men and women, young and old and those with disabilities).[6] And finally, Acts shows how the church is united through the power of the Holy Spirit, which enables all to take part in the work of God's kingdom and to lead people to Christ.

In Acts 1:12–14, Luke identifies some female disciples and Mary the mother of Jesus. The women that were also Christ's followers and Jesus's family members played a vital role in Luke's campaign to promote the disciples' leadership status. This paper argues that Mary and Jesus's brothers represent a significant clientele in the Christian community of the early church. The same idea applies to women, young people and people with disabilities. Alexander noted that it may be true that the general status of these people in the first century was not necessarily equal with that of able men. There is enough evidence to suggest that the female disciples command an unofficial representation of the female audience in Luke-Acts or the Christian community.[7]

Stott observes that the Pentecost event is the final act of saving humanity through the ministry of Jesus Christ before the parousia. What happened at Pentecost brought to the disciples the confidence they needed for their special role in witnessing about God's kingdom on earth. Pentecost is the inauguration of the new era being led by the Spirit.[8] More so, Holladay notes that the coming of the Holy Spirit in Acts 2 shows the effect on the gathered community of believers and even the crowd that were present.[9] Scholars like Holladay, John Stott, David Williams and James Dunn interpreted the events on the empowering and speaking in various tongues that further lead to the speech

---

6. Longenecker, "Acts of the Apostles," 217.
7. Alexander, *Preface to Luke's Gospel*, 191.
8. John Stott, *Message of Acts*, 60–61.
9. Holladay, *Acts*, 89.

by Peter the leader during the initial stages of the church.[10] Most scholars and commentators also considered the section as the fulfillment of the prophecy in the book of Joel on the disciples of Christ.

In the Roman Empire, where the events of New Testament books are located, people with disabilities often faced several challenges from the time they are born. As Beerden observes,

> the birth of a disabled child was regarded by the Romans as a great misfortune. A high percentage of disabled children were abandoned outdoors immediately after birth and left to die because many Romans felt it was pointless to prolong lives that would prove to be a practical and financial burden on the rest of the family.[11]

People with disabilities were abandoned and discriminated in the family and also in the society because some considered them not to be complete human beings. However, during the early church people with disabilities were part of the followers of Jesus either because they were seeking healing or were part of the new religious movement that gave voice and special attention to them. That is why Dionysius of Halicarnassus discusses how people with disabilities need to be treated right:

> In the first place, he obliged the inhabitants to bring up all their male children and the first-born of the females, and forbade them to destroy any children less than three years of age unless they were maimed or monstrous from their very birth. These he did not forbid their parents to expose, provided they first showed them to their five nearest neighbours and these also approved. Against those who disobeyed this law, he fixed various penalties, including the confiscation of half their property.[12]

Therefore, it is clear that the gospel of Luke makes mention of people with disabilities that are following Jesus Christ for healing, food, teaching, or probably because he welcomes them the way they are without any discrimination. For instance, in Luke 1:26–38 where Zechariah was deaf and still ministering in the temple, and in Luke 5:12–26 where Jesus healed the man with leprosy and the paralytic. In the feeding of the five thousand, in Luke

---

10. See Holladay, *Acts*; Stott, *Message of Acts*; Williams, *Acts*; and Dunn, *Acts of the Apostles*.
11. Beerden, "Are They Monsters," 5.
12. Dionysius of Halicarnassus, *Roman Antiquities* 2.15.2 (Cary, LCL), 354–55.

9:10–17, it is also recorded that Jesus welcomed people and healed those that needed healing as well as fed them. These among other examples show that people with disabilities may be part of those that the Holy Spirit came upon in Acts 2, but to whom most scholars and commentators give less attention. This paper also considers other New Testament texts that show how inclusive the church (every human being) started and that we are all partners in the ministry of God's work, for which the Holy Spirit commissions human beings.

The Church in Acts

The day of Pentecost gives birth to the church (in the New Testament) with the followers of Jesus waiting in Jerusalem for the promised Holy Spirit. The coming down of the Holy Spirit on Pentecost day added to the church thousands of Jews and Gentiles, who were saved in Jerusalem (Acts 2:41, 47; 4:4). A short time later there was another increase in numbers to the church as recorded in Acts 6:7, Luke records that "And the word of God increased, and the number of the disciples multiplied greatly in Jerusalem, and a great many of the priests were obedient to the faith" (RSV). The book discusses the growth of the church from Jerusalem to Rome, the capital of the Roman Empire, and other parts of the world. Acts 8:1 shows how persecution scattered believers from Jerusalem to other places, though previously it appears that they (men, women and people with disabilities) were not ready or willing to spread the gospel to other parts as they were told. Persecution facilitated the spread of the gospel and also the growth of the church. "What some intended to silence Christ's message served rather to speed up the spread of the gospel throughout the Roman Empire. It's likely that is why the church reached Rome even before Paul, the church's greatest missionary, arrived there"[13] (Acts 28:14–15) through the help of the Holy Spirit.

More importantly, Acts shows the beginning of household churches and the coming down of the Holy Spirit on all followers of Jesus. The early church (Acts 1:1–7:60) appears to be strictly dominated by the Jewish people, considering the twelve disciples were all Jews. It is also worth noting that the followers of Jesus Christ are people of different backgrounds – which are all-inclusive, such as people with disabilities because it is possible that Jesus did not heal all those that have disabilities and were following him, as noted above. Women (Mary and Martha, among others) and young people are also part of the followers of Jesus (Mark 10:13–16). Women are among those that listened

---
13. Woods, *Acts*, 18.

and understood to the point of fulfilling Jesus's teaching in the gospels; the feeding of four thousand and five thousand people signify that the followers of Jesus are all-inclusive (Matt 14:15–21; Mark 6:35–44; Luke 9:12–17; John 6:5–15). One can also see the role of young people in the New Testament such as John Mark, Titus and Timothy being leaders of the various churches that were founded.

Reading Acts 2 gives further information about those that were present on the day of Pentecost; travelers from fifteen locations heard the gospel in their various tongues/languages. The early church was inclusive, Hansung Kim notes that in Acts 6:1, the church included two distinct Jewish groups: one Hebrews (Jews), the other Hellenistic Greeks.[14] In Acts 8:1–40, we find Philip reaching beyond the Jews, preaching to Samaritans and later to an Ethiopian man. Furthermore, "Acts 10 brings a notable shift in this pattern. Here, God specifically instructs Peter to share the gospel with Cornelius, an important officer in Rome's hated military."[15] The vision in Acts 10:9–23 is a call to inclusion of everyone God created irrespective of gender, race and nationality. This led to a change of attitude toward non-Jews/Gentiles, which shows the inclusion of other people and not only Jews through the leadership of the Holy Spirit. This is the fulfillment of what God has said right from the Old Testament (Joel 2:28–29)[16] that the outpouring of the Spirit will be on all human beings, which is inclusive and not exclusive when it comes to gender, age and ability.

The interpretation (Acts 2:1–42) which only focuses on speaking in tongues continues to separate people within the church and tends to deny the role of the Holy Spirit when it comes to partnership of all people in the church – even though the walls of disparities (Acts 2:8–11) are something that the outpouring of the Holy Spirit dealt with, showing that all human beings are equal in the eyes of God and all can be partners in the ministry (ordained). The coming of the Holy Spirit gave the followers of Jesus (men and women, young and old, and people with disabilities) the boldness to preach the Word to everyone, the message of salvation, in other words commission every believer for the work of God. Acts 11:19–21 describes how many of those who had been scattered by the persecution spread the word only to Jews, but some began to speak also to the Greeks in Antioch bringing to fulfillment of the word of God.[17] One

---

14. Kim, "Rereading Acts 6:1–7."
15. Wood, *Acts*, 18.
16. Blackburn, "Holy Spirit in Luke-Acts."
17. Wood, *Acts*, 18.

finds the call of Paul and his commissioning (Acts 9) to the Gentile world as another shift in the way some of the Jews perceived salvation of humanity. Acts 13 sees another decisive movement as Paul turns to the Gentiles when the Jews in Pisidian Antioch reject the Gospel (Acts 13:43–47).[18] Gradually the population of the church increased and included people from different tribes, nations, languages, young and old, men and women and people from different cultures. There are female disciples in Acts 9:32–43 such as Dorcas who also preached through her good deeds to the widows.

More so, the book of Acts also deals with the partnership in the ministry of men and women who became believers (Acts 5:14) and this also includes people with disabilities. The principle of self-agency in the salvation of women is shown further with the distinction that men and women are spoken of individually as being baptized (Acts 8:12). There are women, such as Mary, who happen to be instrumental in providing her house as a meeting place for the church (Acts 12:12). There is also Lydia who became a believer and her entire family were baptized (Acts 16:11–15).[19] Priscilla and Aquila are seen to be involved in the correction of Apollos, seemingly Priscilla was mentioned first which gives her the prominent position in the act of correcting Apollos (Acts 18:24, 26). This shows how the church was a ministry of partnership that is inclusive of all believers in Christ being led by the Holy Spirit irrespective of age, gender, nationality, race and ethnic group, among other things that cause division in the churches in Nigeria.

The church in Acts is not merely a community of those who believe in Jesus as their master and Lord. The church is much more than that, through the early believers' acts of showing love their numbers keep growing. When one becomes a member of the church, one becomes part of a family, which in the book of Acts started as a household of God. Christopher Stenschke postulates that the household serves as space where they meet and devote themselves to instruction (apostles' teaching) and fellowship, to the breaking of bread (Eucharist) and prayer (Acts 2:42). They pray for boldness (4:29), share their possessions to help those in need (4:32–37) and heal the sick and suffering (5:15–16), all while facing great persecution (5:40–41), for which they rejoice.[20] The early Christian community was a dynamic fellowship of preachers and practitioners, in which men and women are partners in the ministry, and the more the community preaches and practices, the more the community grows.

---

18. Wood, *Acts*, 18.
19. Dale, "Dismantling Socio-Sacred Hierarchy," 21.
20. Stenschke, "Mission," 75.

There is no discrimination in the early church, even the incident that happened in Acts 6 was resolved so that all would be catered for and no one or group left out. Most importantly, the church in Acts is united by a common mission and goal that the coming of the Holy Spirit helped in accomplishing through the partnership of men, women, young, old and people with disabilities in the household churches.

The Nigerian Church

The church in Nigeria (evangelicals) appears to be dominated by traditional and patriarchal interpretations of the Bible, which appear to be driven by culture. It is imperative to say that the evangelical churches in Nigeria were planted by missionaries that came from different cultures and contexts. Harvey Sindima notes that the missionaries brought other baggage with them; they also identified Christianity with their culture, values and history. The result of such uncritical appropriation of cultural views made Christianity an ideology of Western civilization. Being a cultural ideology, it was used by both the colonialist and the missionary alike to promote cultural superiority.[21]

Reading the Bible within the African context is not a monolithic phenomenon but rather a polylithic one. That is why Justin Ukpong expresses that reading the Bible in the African context, with its diversities and complexities, is a challenging process.[22] This research observes that the interpretation of the Bible and the Nigerian culture contribute to the complexity of inclusion of both genders among evangelical churches. The church in Nigeria also grew out of such an environment where most of the traditions of the Nigerian people have been cemented through the patriarchal interpretation of the Christian faith, especially understandings of gender. Christianity is believed to be growing faster in Nigeria than in any other country in Africa.[23] Ukpong further states that because of its ambivalence, the Bible can be put to different uses. The reason may be that the message seems to be addressing some issues the continent is facing, even though some use such avenues to exploit the people of their money. All these are due to the misinterpretation of the Bible. It is important to note that women and young people dominate the high population in the evangelical churches in Nigeria. Nevertheless, it appears that the inclusion of women, young people and people with disabilities

---

21. Sindima, *Drums of Redemption*, 117.
22. Ukpong, "New Testament Hermeneutics," 152.
23. Aigbadumah, "Jesus the Healer," 3; see also Okoli and Okwuosa, "Role of Christianity."

in leadership (ordained) is a struggle for most denominations, especially the evangelical churches in Nigeria (such as ECWA, COCIN, Anglican and ERCC).

A substantial number of evangelical churches in Nigeria still use a patriarchal and cultural interpretation of the Bible to deny, subordinate and oppress young people, women and people with disabilities when it comes to partnership in ministry and leadership. The use of a Eurocentric interpretation is also contributing to lack of equal partnership in ministry. Many of the women within the above-named churches accept the ideology that they are not called into the ministry. Kanyoro rightly argues that, "women by their gender, often experience discrimination in terms of denial of equal access to decision-making positions in church and society. Discrimination promotes the uneconomical use of women's talents, creates feelings of low esteem and worthlessness."[24] Such a situation applies to young people, people with disabilities and those from different tribes or ethnic groups to those in the leadership positions, meaning that ordination and partnering in ministry within the evangelical churches in Nigeria is very difficult.

Similarly, John Bwire observes that the traditional cultures within Africa have been the common obstacle and the cause of discrimination against women, young people and people with disabilities.[25] In most traditions in Nigeria, men are considered to be leaders, kings and chiefs, they are the key people when it comes to decision-making in society. This appears to be having strongholds when it comes to the interpretation of the Bible in the above-named churches. More so, Bwire agrees that Christian leaders in Nigeria have a biblical text to turn to that can help bolster the place of women, young people, and people with disabilities in the church that is not exclusive. But men who are the majority still choose to interpret the Bible in a way that will deprive women, young people and people with disabilities of their God-given talents and gifts.[26] The culture of Nigeria, which appears to give no room for women, young people and people with disabilities, contributes to the oppressiveness and lack of diverse inclusion in decision-making. Furthermore, theological misinterpretation of the Bible has exhilarated centuries-old gender injustices and inequalities that have denied the recognition of women in roles and development within the church and society. This misinterpretation of biblical texts forms the basis for

---

24. Musimbi R. A. Kanyoro, "God Calls to Ministry: An Inclusive Hospitality," in *Groaning in Faith: African Women in the Household of God*. Edited by Musimbi R.A. Kanyoro and Nyambura J. Njoroge (Nairobi, Kenya: Action Publishers, 1996), 151.

25. Bwire, "Practicing Biblical Equity," 182.

26. Bwire, 185.

justifying inequality and injustice against women within Nigeria and rests on the misapplication of a societal construction of gender roles when it comes to leadership and ministry.

Many churches in Nigeria preach an inclusive gospel but find it difficult to link that with an inclusive church. For instance, they preach that people are created in the image and likeness of God, but when it comes to comprehensive partnership in ministry the reverse is the case. The young people, women and people with disabilities are crying out for full inclusion in the church. There cannot be full partnership unless the church reevaluates and changes the traditions and structures that tend to relegate these people, especially women, to the home.[27] Many of such churches only interpret the events in Acts concerning speaking in tongues, or passages in Pauline letters such as first Timothy 2:12 and first Corinthians 11:5, among others. These passages appear to be interpreted through patriarchal and cultural lenses and are used to deny women and people with disabilities inclusion in the ministry of the Word. The young people are considered not to be ready for leadership or too young for such a task. People with disabilities are treated as lesser human beings in most cases, and most churches tend to act as if the Holy Spirit cannot work through them when it comes to partnership in ministry. This is similar to what Chemorion observes that,

> to make good sense of the Bible, a reader must pay attention to both the cultural and literary contexts of the text. However, the reader's cultural worldview may also lead to misinterpretation of the text, especially when biblical ideas are misread as being identical with what is found in the reader's local culture.[28]

Inclusive Rereading of Acts 2:1–47 for Partnership in Ministry

The day of Pentecost represents the first harvest of Jesus's followers since the age of the Spirit has come. "When the day of Pentecost came, they were all together in one place" as recorded in Acts 2:1. Furthermore, Acts 1:15 states about 120 people were in the upstairs room, it is also possible that it was the room where Jesus ate the Last Supper with his disciples (Luke 22:12). The group in the upper rom included the eleven disciples, other people who had followed Jesus from the beginning of his earthly ministry (like Matthias and Joseph) and women

---

27. Kanyoro, 151.
28. Chemorion, "Created Equal," 32–33.

(Luke 23:55–56). Those among the crowd also include Jesus's mother Mary and his brothers, James and Jude. They were praying and waiting for the Holy Spirit to come as Jesus promised (John 14:15–17). Pentecost places prominence on the unifying power of the Holy Spirit on everyone that follows Christ. Human beings (men, women, young and old, people with disability) "numbering about a hundred and twenty" persons (Acts 1:14–15) were all "together" (Acts 2:1). Gilbert Bilezikian avers that the whirlwind sound surrounded *all the people* who were the recipients of the Holy Spirit with a living flame. This enablement meant not only that the Spirit was giving them new powers to proclaim the gospel in all the world but also, and more importantly, that the human race was again being united into one body.[29]

Reading Acts 2:1, it is imperative that the phrase ἦσαν πάντες ὁμοῦ "they were all together" signifies that all of the disciples of Jesus (all-inclusive of human beings that were present) were together waiting for the descending of the Holy Spirit. The verb ἦσαν, which is a third-person plural meaning "they," and the adjective πάντες, which refers to "all, the whole, every kind of," gives an impression of being an inclusive gathering and not exclusive as most of the traditional interpretations suggest. Therefore the Holy Spirit came upon all the followers of Christ that were gathered in the upper room in Jerusalem. The empowerment of the Holy Spirit is on all as stated in Joel 2:28–29 where the similar Greek adjective ὅλον (all, the whole, entire, complete) is used to qualify the inclusive nature of the people present when they were filled with the Holy Spirit on the day of Pentecost.

Therefore, the Holy Spirit came upon them irrespective of gender, age and race. The coming down of the Holy Spirit in Acts 2:1–47 gives believers the boldness to be partners in the ministry of the Word, to which God calls all of humanity. The early church recognized that and also showed how they partner with all believers even in leadership even though not everything is recorded in the Acts of the Apostles. The church spread like a fire across the Roman Empire. The Spirit is the key to helping each believer be a partner and to view all people as created in the image and likeness of God. Acts serves at least four primary functions in the New Testament as noted by George Wood;

> First, Acts serves as a bridge between the Gospels and Paul's letters, which needs to be read and understood from the purpose of the church. Second, Acts tells how the church grew in numbers, geographically, in the cultural scope of its mission, and theology.

---

29. Bilezikian, *Beyond Sex Roles*, 91–93.

Third, Acts serves as a guide for faith and apology. Fourth, Luke emphasizes the power of the Holy Spirit. If we miss Luke's emphasis on the Holy Spirit, we miss the greatest purpose in writing the book.[30]

Equally, Kanyoro alludes that the early church provides a model for Christian mutuality where everyone participated in spreading the message of Christ including taking up leadership positions.[31]

Similarly important to this paper with regards to partnership in ministry is the Greek word κοινωνία. According to Phemelo Marumo this refers to a partnership, contributory help, participation, sharing in, communion, and fellowship in the Spirit.[32] The word (κοινωνία) will be used in this article to mean "partnership" in the ministry that God calls all human beings to, which also includes taking up leadership roles when the need arises. The word is used in Acts 2:42 and is key to this study. As Norman Bull affirms, the word is used to refer to the Christian community because they are a group of people that are sharing, helping each other and living a common life.[33] It is about the practice of collective responsibility and understanding that God calls all people irrespective of gender and ability. *Koinonia* in ministry speaks about the partnership that is lived out in the experience of shared power and responsibility. Ministerial formation in Acts embraces a theology of partnership through the Holy Spirit that enables the early church to provide a model for the church in Nigeria. The early church model is on shared responsibilities and accountability between its leaders and its people.[34] The church in Nigeria should learn from the model of the early church, which through the leadership of the Holy Spirit enabled them to do works for the kingdom of God irrespective of their diversities. Diversity can be seen as part of God's plan, that works through the Holy Spirit and the church to overcome barriers and boundaries, as seen in the book of Acts. Kanyoro further argues that

> Partnership should delight in and recognize the richness of diversity. Partnership depends on mutuality and respecting the image of God in the person. Giving and receiving are the hand and glove of partnership. In mutual relationships, each party brings

---

30. Wood, *Acts*, 21.
31. Kanyoro, 155.
32. Marumo, "Reconciliation in South Africa," 2.
33. Bull, *Rise of the Church*, 113.
34. Kanyoro, 156.

something of value, each receives something of worth and the mutual exchange is recognized and respected by both.[35]

The church in Nigeria needs to see the partnership in ministry when the Holy Spirit came down in Acts 2:1–47. Such partnership can only come out of a willing heart to accept the role of the Holy Spirit and through inner conviction and love to know that all human beings are created in the image of God and so the Holy Spirit can work in all. That is why Kanyoro asserts that "partnership in ministry should challenge the understanding of the gospel and specifically the message of Christ's death, resurrection and ascension . . . partnership calls us to affirm others whom tradition has side-lined for years."[36] When the Christian church in Nigeria recognizes that God created people to partner in the ministry irrespective of gender, age, ability or disability, then the church through the leadership of the Holy Spirit will grow, just like the one in Acts. The partnership takes place around a task of service in which *koinonia* is important to the evangelical churches in Nigeria as a gift of the Holy Spirit that focuses on Christ who sets people free from the oppression, exploitation and denial of using their leadership qualities to serve God.

When the followers of Christ received the Holy Spirit on the day of Pentecost all the believers in the upper room were filled and received boldness. This event defined the distinctive nature of the new community (church) as a body where oneness and, therefore, equality prevailed since, in Christ Jesus, those who were far from one another have been brought near. Breaking down the dividing wall of hostility, division and disregard based on age, gender and ability, God created new people with the shared responsibility of spreading the message of salvation. All believers have been reconciled in one body, thereby bringing the hostility to an end (Eph 2:13–16). The book of Acts celebrates newness of life through the ideal community of partnership, mutuality in equality in the work of God.

Peter's appropriation of Joel's prophecy should govern the Nigerian church's understanding of inclusion of women, young people and those with disabilities in partnerships in the ministry of the Word. The Holy Spirit is given to "*all flesh*" (Acts 2:42). Therefore, all human beings can be used by God and called by God into the ministry either full time or part time. For instance, there were women who served as coworkers with Paul such as Phoebe, Persis, Priscilla and Julia, among others (Romans 16:1–16). In this new community of believers,

---

35. Kanyoro, 156.
36. Kanyoro, 156.

gender and hierarchal distinctions centered on age and ability were removed so that anyone could be used as a channel to provide divine guidance and serve God. We see the likes of Timothy and Titus as young people who were involved in the leadership of the church. The Holy Spirit has closed the generational gap and this should serve as a lesson for the evangelical churches in Nigeria.

Conclusion

This article was able to show how the church can partner in ministry just like the church in Acts. The Holy Spirit played a major role and the early followers of Christ allowed the Holy Spirit to work in them and bring the growth that was experienced in the early church. The evangelical churches in Nigeria should embrace partnership in ministry where it is more of inclusivity than exclusivity. The interpreter of the Bible within the context of Nigeria needs to consider the world around the text, especially in interpreting Acts 2:1–47 that shows the people in the upper room included men and women, young and old, and people with disabilities. There is also need to emphasize the context of the Bible and its author as well as the context of the reader and its application to the evangelical churches in Nigeria to embrace partnership in ministry of the Word. Knowing that God made all of humanity in his image and likeness, God can use anyone at any time for his glory.

Bibliography

Aigbadumah, C. A. "Jesus the Healer: A Theological Reflection on the Role of Christology in the Growth of the Mountain of Fire and Miracles Church in Nigeria." PhD thesis, Vrije Universiteit, Amsterdam, 2011. Available online, https://research.vu.nl/en/publications/jesus-the-healer-a-theological-reflection-on-the-role-of-christol, 1–25.

Alexander, Loveday C. A. *The Preface to Luke's Gospel: Literary Convention and Social Context in Luke 1:1–4 and Acts 1:1*. Cambridge: Cambridge University Press, 1993.

Beerden, K. "Are They Monsters or Entertainment? The Position of the Disabled in the Roman Empire." MA thesis, Leiden University, 20 September 2017.

Bilezikian, Gilbert. *Beyond Sex Roles: What the Bible Says about a Woman's Place in Church and Family*. 3rd ed. Grand Rapids: Baker Academic, 2006.

Blackburn, Barry L. "The Holy Spirit in Luke-Acts: A Survey." *Leaven* 5, no. 2, article 4 (1997). Available online, http://digitalcommons.pepperdine.edu/leaven/vol5/iss2/4.

Bull, Norman J. *The Rise of the Church*. London: Heinemann Educational, 1967.

Bwire, John Peter. "Practicing Biblical Equity in African Society." In *The Quest for Gender Equity in Leadership*, edited by Keumju Jewel Hyun and Diphus C. Chemorion, 180–96. Eugene: Wipf & Stock, 2016.

Chemorion, Diphus C. "Created Equal: A Fresh Look at Gender Equity in Genesis 1–3." In *The Quest for Gender Equity in Leadership*, edited by Keumju Jewel Hyun and Diphus C. Chemorion, 31–41. Eugene: Wipf & Stock, 2016.

Dale, Moyra. "Dismantling Socio-Sacred Hierarchy: Gender and Gentiles in Luke-Acts." *Priscilla Papers* 31, no. 2 (Spring 2017): 19–23. https://www.cbeinternational.org/sites/default/files/05-dismantling.pdf.

Dibelius, Martin. *The Book of Acts*. Minneapolis: Fortress Press, 2004.

Dionysius of Halicarnassus. *Roman Antiquities, Volume I: Books 1–2*. Translated by Earnest Cary. Loeb Classical Library 319. Cambridge: Harvard University Press, 1937.

Dunn, James. *Acts of the Apostles*. London: Epworth Press, 1996.

Holladay, Carl R. *Acts: A Commentary*. Louisville: Westminster John Knox Press, 2016.

Kanyoro, Musimbi R.A. "God Calls to Ministry: An Inclusive Hospitality," in *Groaning in Faith: African Women in the Household of God*. Edited by Musimbi R.A. Kanyoro and Nyambura J. Njoroge. Nairobi, Kenya: Action Publishers, 1996. 149–60.

Kim, Hansung. "Rereading Acts 6:1–7: Lessons for Multicultural Mission Organizations." *Missio Nexus*, posted 1 January 2009. https://missionexus.org/rereading-acts-61-7-lessons-for-multicultural-mission-organizations/.

Longenecker, Richard. "Acts of the Apostles." In *The Expositor's Bible Commentary: New Testament*, edited by Frank E. Gaebelein. Grand Rapids: Zondervan, 1984.

Marumo, P. O. "Reconciliation in South Africa in Light of the Imago Dei and Koinonia." *Verbum et Ecclesia* 40, no. 1 (2019): 1–10. https://doi.org/10.4102/ve.v40i1.1905.

Oduyoye, Mercy Amba. *Daughters of Anowa: African Women and Patriarchy*. Maryknoll: Orbis Books, 1995.

Okoli, A. B., and L. Okwuosa. "The Role of Christianity in Gender Issues and Development in Nigeria." *HTS Teologiese Studies* 76, no. 4 (2020): 1–8. https://doi.org/10.4102/hts.v76i4.6007.

Sindima, Harvey J. *Drums of Redemption: An Introduction to African Christianity*. Westport: Greenwood Press, 1994.

Stenschke, Christopher. "Mission in the Book of Acts: Mission of the Church." *Scriptura* 103 (2010): 66–78.

Stott, John R. W. *The Message of Acts*. Downers Grove: InterVarsity Press, 1994.

Ukpong, Justin S. "New Testament Hermeneutics in Africa: Challenges and Possibilities." *Neotestamentica* 35, nos. 1–2 (2001): 147–67.

Williams, David J. *Acts*. Grand Rapids: Baker Books, 2011.

Wood, George O. *Acts: The Holy Spirit at Work in Believers*. 3rd ed. Springfield: Global University, 2010.

2

A Comparison of the Montanists and the Pentecostals in Their Expression of the Reception of the Holy Spirit in Christian History

Kwaku Boamah

Lecturer in Early Church History, University of Ghana, Legon, Ghana

and

Jacob Kwame Opata

Graduate Student, Trinity Theological Seminary and Associate Pastor, ICGC Military Temple, Legon, Ghana

Abstract

The reception of a new religious movement is usually met with resistance both within and outside the larger group. The emergence of the Montanist in the mid-second century and the Pentecostal movements from the early twentieth century faced a lot of confrontation within the Christian fold. Interestingly, the two movements stressed the character of God's Spirit in Christian beliefs and expressions, as they felt the Spirit's absence or minimization in Christian expressions. To demonstrate the way they were accommodated, the history of these movements and their main characteristics are compared to show why they were resisted by the existing church in their days. In this paper, the usage of Scripture, future expectations and methods of life, particularly the position of women, are compared between Montanists and Pentecostals in order to highlight their parallels and distinctions. The study discovers that, despite being at different eras in the church annals, the two Christian movements share many similarities, confirming the adage that there is nothing new under the sun. The study sustains that the character and works of the Spirit in the church are often resisted, but the Spirit has always found a way to be prominent.

Key words: charismatics, heresy, Montanism, Pentecostalism, Spirit

Introduction

Although we often claim novelty to developments, Ecclesiastes 1:9–10 posits that

> that which has been is what will be, that which is done is what will be done, and there is nothing new under the sun. Is there anything of which it may be said, "See, this is new?" It has already been in ancient times before us. (NKJV)

It is almost always true that a careful examination of modern practices reveals superficial differences and fundamental similarities existing between some new movements and ancient types. This observation seems true when charismatic expressions in the church are examined through the lens of history, from the early church period to the twentieth century.

There was an early church charismatic movement called the Montanist or the New Prophesy, which was later branded as heretic by the church at the time due to their modus operandi.[1] The movement grew, drawing large numbers of people, but posed challenges to the existing ecclesiastical order because of their zeal and apocalyptic ideologies.[2] The movement stressed the participation of the Spirit in the church's activities. The Montanists' movement shares some similarities with Pentecostal movements that emerged in Africa at the dawn of the twentieth century. At the emergence of the Pentecostal movements, the historical mainline churches did not take their activities kindly due to their mode of expression, character and form of service.

---

1. Grayson, "Montanism and the Empire," 87; Kim "Is Montanism a Heretical Sect," 113.
2. Oshitelu, *African Fathers*, 150.

This study suggests that the character and activities of the early church period Montanists and the twentieth-century Pentecostal movement are more similar than different. Omenyo argues strongly that there are equivalents between the Montanists of the early church and the Pentecostal movements today since they both arose within the church because they focused on the participation of the Spirit in God's church.[3] Notwithstanding, although Kim affirms the question he asks in his title *Is Montanism a Heretical Sect or Pentecostal Antecedent?*, he does not compare the activities of the Montanists to the twentieth-century Pentecostal movement properly.[4]

This study, therefore, examines in a comparative and historical approach, the charismatic expressions, or the place and function of the Spirit, among Montanists in the annals of the church to the present-day Pentecostal movement in Ghana. The study clusters together the various trends of the charismatic and Pentecostal categories in contemporary times as the Pentecostal movement into a single entity since their expressions are the same with regards to the function and position of the Spirit; in contrast to the historical mainline churches in Ghana, since they are believed to put less emphasis on the Spirit. Though the historical mainline churches believe in the Spirit, expressions associated with the Spirit are not consciously promoted and demonstrated routinely at their services.

Aside from comparing the two groups, the study looks at how existing churches accommodated them at the time of their emergence. The aim is to evaluate the similarities and differences between the Montanist and Pentecostals, concerning their expression of the *charismata*, use of scriptures, the doctrine of the end time, way of life and the role of women in these movements, among other comparative elements, which differentiated them from the existing churches at the time of their emergence.

The work, therefore, traces the position and function of the Spirit in church annals, from the apostolic days to the patristic era through the Azusa experience to modern times. Furthermore, the characteristics of the Montanist and Pentecostal movements are compared, including the historical records of how they were received by the existing church at the time they appeared.

---

3. Omenyo, *Pentecost outside Pentecostalism*, 79.
4. Kim, "Is Montanism a Heretical Sect," 124.

Pentecostalism and *Charismata* in the New Testament Church

The origin of the church, after the ascension, connects strongly to the Pentecost experience in Acts 2. The apostle Peter, full of the Spirit, commenting on the experience of communicating in strange languages – accompanying the reception of the Spirit, by the one hundred and twenty disciples in the upper room – referred to the prophecy of Joel 2:28, which instantly attracted about three thousand more into their fold. Peter interpreted the manifestation of the Spirit who aided them to speak in the native languages of the audience as the fulfillment of that which was spoken by Joel.

Furthermore, as a way of exhorting and pointing the people to Christ, Peter portrayed the manifestation of the gifts as a phenomenon that will continue in subsequent generations. In Acts 2:38–39, Peter instructed his audience, saying,

> Repent, and let every one of you be baptized in the name of Jesus Christ for the remission of sins; and you shall receive the gift of the Spirit. *For the promise is to you and your children, and to all who are afar off, as many as the Lord our God will call.*[5]

Peter's interpretation connects manifestations of the gifts of the Spirit in church annals and the fulfillment of Joel's prophecy. Therefore, one may read about churches in Corinth, Galatia, and in other places exercising and sometimes, "abusing" the gifts of the Spirit (e.g. 1 Cor 12:1–31). Individuals like Timothy and Titus were also encouraged to discover more about the gift endowed to them by the Spirit. Timothy, in particular, was urged by Paul to stir the gifts (2 Tim 1:6–7). The gifts were therefore important in the mission and work of the early Christians. However, the era after the passing of the apostles saw a decline in the manifestation of the activities of the Spirit.[6] Omenyo points to the "cessation of the charismata Theory" which suggests that "the charismata ceased after the death of the last Apostle."[7] The main proponents advocate that the manifestations ended with the apostles, canonization of Scripture or other formal structures of the church.[8] Hence, belief and demonstration of such gifts were looked upon with suspicion, frowned on and sometimes forbidden. Therefore, various groups and movements that have arisen with a claim of experiencing the presence of the Spirit are subjected to various

---

5. NKJV, emphasis added.
6. Cox, *Fire from Heaven*, 47.
7. Omenyo, *Pentecost outside Pentecostalism*, 77.
8. Reymond, *What About Continuing Revelations*, 32–34. See also Gentry, *Charismatic Gift of Prophecy*, 31–33; MacArthur, *Charismatics*, 165–66; Gaffin, *Perspectives on Pentecost*, 109.

degrees of opposition, especially within the confines of the church – like the reception of the Montanists in the early church as well as the Pentecostals from the twentieth century. Some scholars have, however, written about the gifts affirming their operations in the present-day church, just as the gifts operated in the days of the apostles.[9]

The Montanist Movement

The Montanists are largely described as a charismatic group of Christians who emphasized the role of the Spirit, particularly prophecy, as a Christian expression. Omenyo describes them as the "fountainhead" of charismatics in Christian history, although he possibly should have qualified it as after the apostolic era.[10] His description shows their earliest reception after the Acts 2 experience. The origin of this movement may be traced to the latter part of the second century. Trevett initially indicated that it started not later than AD 160, where it rose to significance.[11] However, she dates their origin back to AD 150. This date is generally accepted by other scholars such as Grayson and Denzey.[12] However, Robeck traces the movement to the later part of the second century, while Muzzey agrees it was started in the middle of the second century.[13] Thus, Montanism may be said to have risen to significance within the second half and later period of the second century.

It is further believed to have started in Phrygia and Asia Minor and spread to other parts of the Roman Empire rapidly; a claim that has been corroborated by Muzzey, Grayson and Robecks.[14] However, Denzey advocates Pepouza as its place of origin, which is not sustained because Pepouza later emerged as the spiritual headquarters of the movement.[15]

---

9. Hollenweger, *Pentecostalism*. See also Anderson, *Moya*; Cox, *Fire from Heaven*; Asamoah-Gyadu, *African Charismatics*.
10. Omenyo, *Pentecost outside Pentecostalism*, 78.
11. Trevett, "Montanism," 929.
12. Grayson, "Montanism and the Empire," 87; Denzey, "What Did the Montanists Read?" 429.
13. Robeck, "Montanism and Present Day Prophets," 413–29; Muzzey, "Spiritual Franciscans Montanist Heretics?" 588–608.
14. Trevett, "Gender, Authority and Church History," 9; Muzzey, "Spiritual Franciscans Montanist Heretics?" 601; Grayson, "Montanism and the Empire," 87; Robeck, "Montanism and Present-Day Prophets," 413.
15. Denzey, "What Did the Montanists Read?" 429.

The movement was called "the New Prophecy" or "the Prophecy."[16] Other critics refer to the movement as the "Phrygian" or "Cataphrygian" heresies.[17] Some prominent members of the Montanist movement included Perpetua and her companions who were martyred by the Governor Hilarianus.[18] The other was Tertullian, the early Latin African father from Carthage. Tertullian withdrew from the fellowship of the African church and joined Montanism for a period.[19] He later moved from the movement to form his sect, which was called Tertullianistae.[20] Omenyo suggests that Tertullian joined the Montanist movement as a result of the way the group emphasized the position and function of the Spirit in Christian expression and their ascetic way of living.[21]

The most prominent name of the movement used as a description was Montanist, derived from the name of its generally agreed founder Montanus, formerly a priest of the cult of Cybele.[22] There were two other women associated with Montanus who played significant roles, Priscilla and Maximilla. Trevett argued that Priscilla was the most significant of the three forerunners of the movement and Montanus as the "paraclete," the "advocate" for the women.[23] Priscilla is often ridiculed for her claim of being a virgin since she was married before her association with the Montanist movement.[24] Trevett has written of the fact that scholars do not agree on how Montanus and Maximilla died.[25] It is nevertheless agreed that when the three (Montanus, Maximilla and Priscilla) died, they were buried at Pepouza, their spiritual and administrative headquarters.[26] Trevett further cites Jeane Anne, who intimates that the name Montanist, associated with the same movement, may have been designated, assigned and informed by male "supremacists" since the women played more significant roles than Montanus himself.[27]

---

16. Lynch, *Early Christian World*, 76.
17. Trevett, "Montanism," 868; Lynch, *Early Christian World*, 76.
18. Musurillo, "Martyrdom of Perpetua," 4:1; Boamah, *Magic and Obstinacy*, 45, 124; Trevett, "Montanism," 941.
19. Denzey, "What Did the Montanists Read?" 431; Lynch, *Early Christian World*, 78.
20. Trevett, "Montanism," 929, 941–43.
21. Omenyo, *Pentecost outside Pentecostalism*, 80.
22. Lynch, *Early Christian World*, 76; Trevett, "Gender, Authority and Church History," 10.
23. Trevett, "Montanist," 937.
24. Trevett, 938.
25. Trevett, 938.
26. Lynch, *Early Christian World*, 77; Trevett, "Montanist," 936.
27. Trevett, "Gender, Authority and Church History," 11.

There are several issues and factors that have been noted to have caused the rise and emergence of Montanism. First, Montanism was a reaction to Gnosticism.[28] The growing rate of Gnosticism among the early Christians in the Roman Empire was fast. The Gnostics were rather more interested in knowledge, whereas the Montanists felt the Spirit was more important as the basis for Christian action than knowledge. The Montanists maintained that knowledge is aided by the Spirit. Therefore, more attention should be focused on the Spirit instead. Montanism consequently stood against a development that sought to render the Christian message as a moral and intellectual one.

Second, the movement rose against some laxities such as low moral standards prevalent in the church, as is evident in the movement's activities and restrictions. Justo L. Gonzalez argues, as maintained by Omenyo earlier on, that the main reasons why Tertullian left the Catholic Church at the time to become a Montanist were largely due to the high moral standards of the Montanists, which were believed to be compromised in the church.[29] Gonzalez noted the rigor in their code of ethics.[30] It is difficult for members to obtain forgiveness, remarry, mingle with the secular and also abstain from martyrdom. The high ethical and moral standards advocated by the Montanists defined their identity and were sometimes even ridiculed by other Christians.

Third, Grayson sees apocalyptic and eschatological concerns as one of the reasons for the rise of the group.[31] They held a strong apocalyptic and eschatological view, which was so eminent they emphasized that Christians should desert the pleasures and comforts of this life. They felt the church at the time was quite self-indulgent in the world, and that it was laying structures as if the world would escape its impending doom and destruction.

Fourth, Montanism arose in response to the church's lack of *charismata*.[32] It is not to say that there was no demonstration of the *charismata*; nonetheless, the emphasis was placed more on order, liturgy and the emerging structures of the church. The use of *charismata* was not routinized as is evident of the Montanists. Since this is the main import of the study, the discussions will be explored later in detail.

Additionally, there were other socio-political issues like martyrdoms, which also served as a background for the rise of the movement. Whereas the

---

28. Oshitelu, *African Fathers*, 160.
29. Gonzalez, *History of Christian Thought*, 172.
30. Gonzalez, 142.
31. Grayson, "Montanism and the Empire," 85–91.
32. Omenyo, *Pentecost Outside Pentecostalism*, 79.

Montanists favored voluntary martyrdom, the Catholic Church opposed such acts. As such suspected Christians had to escape for their lives and at other times, Christians who recanted were accepted back into the Christian fold. One may therefore agree with Trevett that the factors stated above influenced the emergence of Montanism.[33]

Pentecostal Movements

The Pentecostal and charismatic movements are generally classified as part of the worldwide Pentecostal movements.[34] These are movements found in Christianity that mostly focus on the individual's experience of God vis-à-vis the Spirit's baptism. In Ghana, they are distinguished from the historical mainline churches through their understanding of the experience and expression of the Spirit. They understand and view the baptism of the Spirit as an encounter that is separate from conversion. This second encounter enables one to live the Christian life and enjoy all its benefits.[35] Through the second encounter, one becomes endowed with grace, *charisma* and its numerous expressions within Pentecostal circles.

The movement started in the early twentieth century and is traced to the Holiness movements of the time. This Holiness movement maintained extreme Christian positions. Members of the Holiness movements, kept alive by revivalism, lived in anticipation of the immediate parousia of the Christ. Considered to be living in the last times, adherents hoped for God's new outpouring, which would spiritually renew the Christian and bring about the restoration of all things, as promised in Scripture. The outpouring, furthermore, enhanced missions and evangelism to the world in an unprecedented way. Charles Parham, an American influential preacher, who happened to be part of this movement, drew the attention of his congregants through his teachings on the subject of speaking in tongues in 1900.[36]

However, it was William J. Seymour, a black American, who led the three-year-long Azusa Street Revival in Los Angeles, California. The revival resulted in the spread of Pentecostalism throughout the United States and the rest of the world.[37] Most Pentecostal groups, therefore, trace their roots to the Azusa Street

---

33. Trevett, "Montanist," 932.
34. Asamoah-Gyadu, *Sighs and Signs of the Spirit*, 4; Larbi, *Pentecostalism*, 297.
35. Omenyo, *Pentecost outside Pentecostalism*, 86–87.
36. Omenyo, 87–88.
37. Omenyo, 88–90.

Revival. Nonetheless, there is no evidence of the emergence of Pentecostalism in Africa tracing from the Azusa encounter.

Expression of Pentecostalism in Ghana

Given the factors, discussed above, that gave rise to the emergence of the Pentecostal movements, Asamoah-Gyadu posits that the attitude of the historic mission churches to the works, functions and positions of the Spirit in the church, and especially the believer, contributed to the rise of the movement.[38] This shows that, like the Montanist, Pentecostalism emerged when members felt there was a lack of experiential Christianity (which largely points to the expression of the Spirit in Christian living) at the expense of intellectualism. He further submits that the Pentecostal churches have become the choice of Christian expression as a result of three factors.[39] In the first place, it is due to the Pentecostal's stress on personal experience vis-à-vis the Spirit; second, the express manifestation of the Spirit that aids worship; and finally, what he calls the "interventionist nature" of the Spirit that brings healing, breakthrough and deliverance. Initially, theological scholarship in Ghana attempted to associate the movement with Protestantism. However, recent scholarly works by Larbi, Omenyo and Asamoah-Gyadu indicate that the movement in Ghana was not imported but rather was started by natives.[40] Furthermore, though the historical mainline churches were doubtful of the movement, they benefited greatly from the activities of some of these young Pentecostal agents, such as William Wadé Harris and Sampson Oppong, among others.[41]

Scholars such as Asamoah-Gyadu, Omenyo and Larbi have identified major strands or waves of Charismatics in Ghana.[42] The first wave is fondly described as "*Sumsum Sore*" or the African Indigenous Churches (AICs), referring to the activities of several Africans who prophesied. Their charismatic personalities and their campaigns of revival and renewal drew the masses

---

38. Omenyo, 88–90.

39. Asamoah-Gyadu, *Contemporary Pentecostal Christianity*, 6.

40. Omenyo, *Pentecost outside Pentecostalism*, 37; Larbi, *Pentecostalism*, 55; Asamoah-Gyadu, *African Charismatics*, 18–19.

41. Omenyo, *Pentecost outside Pentecostalism*, 67–73.

42. Asamoah-Gyadu, *African Charismatics*, 18–29; Omenyo, *Pentecost outside Pentecostalism*, 93–100; Larbi, *Pentecostalism*, 55–96.

into Christianity.[43] This wave started in 1914 and was led by the Liberian prophet William Wadé Harris. Later, others like prophet Samson Oppong, John Nackabah, Grace Tani and John Swatson were also identified. These are people who expressed charismatic faith in their time, drew a massive following, made converts, demonstrated signs and wonders and were seen as agents of the Spirit. Women were accepted as part of the clergy, and worship was Africanized to meet the needs of the Africans.[44] The organizations that arose, as a result, are known as the "African Independent Churches, African Initiated Churches, African Instituted Churches, or African Indigenous Churches (AICs)."[45]

The second charismatic wave in Ghana is the Western mission-related Pentecostal denominations with indigenous roots, who later became linked with foreign Pentecostal missions. This wave, which may be traced to Peter Anim, started in 1917.[46] Churches identified include the Apostolic Church, Christ Apostolic Church, Church of Pentecost and the Assemblies of God Church. These churches place a strong emphasis on the word of God, healing, prophecy, deliverance, exorcism and evangelism. However, their clergy are mostly male dominated.

The third category of Pentecostals is the renewal groups in the historical mainline churches.[47] These are charismatic groups within the historical mainline churches who want *charismata* but are unwilling to leave their churches. Thus, they try to include charismatic expressions within the traditions of their churches. The role of the charismatic movements in these mainline churches took the form of renewal movements. Certain individuals or groups accepted those charismatic practices and, because it was catching up with many of the members, the church allowed them to operate for various reasons. Omenyo has done a classic analysis of these categories, which include the charismatic renewal in the Roman Catholic Church, the Methodist Prayer and Renewal Program (MPRP) in the Methodist Church Ghana, the Bible Study and Prayer Group (BSPG) in the Presbyterian Church and pockets of charismatic groups

---

43. Christian G. Baëta links the emergence of this movement to the conflicts between European rulers and their subjects. See Baëta, *Prophetism in Ghana*, 2–3; Asamoah-Gyadu, *African Charismatics*, 18–29; Omenyo, *Pentecost outside Pentecostalism*, 37, 67–75; Larbi, *Pentecostalism*, 55–65.

44. Ekem, *Priesthood in Context*.

45. Asamoah-Gyadu, *African Charismatics*, 20.

46. Onyinah, "Pentecostal Exorcism," 123–24.

47. Larbi, *Pentecostalism*, 78–85; Omenyo, *Pentecost outside Pentecostalism*, 93.

in the Anglican Church.⁴⁸ However, today, in the Methodist and Presbyterian churches, their activities have been absorbed by the main church.

Fourth, these groups are referred to as non-denominational revival movements, parachurch organizations and evangelical parachurch movements by Omenyo, Larbi and Adubofuor respectively.⁴⁹ These include religious organizations that are charismatic but are not aligned to any denominational lines. They accept all denominations. This category includes Scripture Union (SU), Ghana Fellowship of Evangelical Students (GHAFES), Women's Aglow, Youth Ambassadors for Christ Association (YAFCA), etc.

The fifth category of the Pentecostal movement is the neo-Pentecostal movements. Omenyo distinguishes between this category and the classical Pentecostal churches by their youthful presence, the excessive use of English and the adoption of the American lifestyle.⁵⁰ Larbi suggests that these churches emerged as a result of the economic and social challenges of the time, which is also agreed upon by Omenyo, so their messages reflect the time, by emphasizing liberation theology or the prosperity gospel.⁵¹

The final category of the Pentecostal movement is the prophetic, which could also be grouped into various categories. These are charismatic movements that emerged in the late 1990s with an emphasis on the prophetic.⁵² To them, it is about being told some secrets of your life. The emphasis here is about demons, witches and other malevolent spirits being the cause of everything. Again, some unorthodox and questionable things are used as elements of this charismatic wave. These things may be anointing oil, lime, porridge, water, etc.⁵³ It is worthy of note that these churches are built strongly around the founders who are often not literate in the English language and yet will be forced to speak for another person to translate. Sometimes, even the interpreter may be worse at the English language than the speaker.

In most cases, they use the media to propagate their ministry. Some own media houses such as TV and radio stations or buy long hours of airtime.⁵⁴ They try to share a lot of testimonies, sometimes doubtful ones, to draw members to

---

48. Omenyo, *Pentecost outside Pentecostalism*, 99–188.
49. Omenyo, 95–96; Larbi, *Pentecostalism*, 86; Adubofuor, "Evangelical Para Church Movement," 1.
50. Omenyo, *Pentecost outside Pentecostalism*, 96.
51. Larbi, *Pentecostalism*, 87; Omenyo, *Pentecost outside Pentecostalism*, 96.
52. Omenyo, *Pentecost outside Pentecostalism*, 96.
53. Omenyo and Atiemo, "Claiming Religious Space," 55–68.
54. Asamoah-Gyadu, *Sighs and Signs of the Spirit*, 27–28.

themselves, and to unintentionally raise suspicions from the populace. Such people rise during a particular period and quickly pass out because many engage in immoral acts and crimes that do not help them to stand the test of time. However, Asamoah-Gyadu uses the expression "neo-Pentecostal" as an umbrella referring to all these groups.[55]

Some of these groups find themselves as independent bodies while others are dependent on and found within existing church structures.[56] One distinctive feature is the association of the charismatic gifts with the ministry. Therefore, individuals who are endowed with spiritual gifts are seen as carriers of the ministry, and sometimes, based on this assumption, people start their own churches. For this paper, the various categories are put together as a Pentecostal movement and contrasted with the Montanist movement.

The following are some of the beliefs and practices. Since they are not the main focus of the study, they are stated summarily. First, they exercise belief in the Bible. Second, they emphasize a charismatic type of leadership where power is concentrated in one person, believed to possess an anointing. However, with time, this was demystified to include a governing body. Third, prophecy is part of the group. Their prophecies are emphatic, with the neo-Pentecostals using prophecies to control what happens in governance, family and individual lives. Fourth, visions and dreams are accepted and used.

The fifth is the belief in healing and deliverance. Sixth is the belief in exorcism. Seventh is the high level of moral ethos, especially among members of the AICs and classical Pentecostals. Eighth, except for the classical Pentecostals, the others allow women to play active roles in the priesthood. Besides, Pentecostals acquired properties and metamorphosed into organizations; some within the structures of the denomination where they developed their faith and others becoming denominations. However, the AICs have either experienced gradual decline, extinction or metamorphosed into prophetic or charismatic churches, by changing their way of doing things.[57]

Finally, they all embraced the use of the media. The western mission-related Pentecostal denomination, charismatic and prophetic churches use the media extensively. They use print, radio, television, the internet and social media for all their work.[58]

---

55. Asamoah-Gyadu, *African Charismatics*, 27.
56. Omenyo, *Pentecost outside Pentecostalism*, 90–98.
57. Asamoah-Gyadu, *African Charismatics*, 30.
58. Asamoah-Gyadu, *Contemporary Pentecostal Christianity*, 11.

A Synthesis

As can be seen in the above, there are major similarities and differences between Montanism and present-day Pentecostal expressions. In the first place, both movements have indigenous roots. They were led by people who did not have sound theological backgrounds and who did not belong to the existing priesthood. Montanus, Peter Anim, William Wadé Harris and the others did not have or undergo any priesthood training or former theological training. Second, the two groups experienced resistance from the established religious circles. Third, the effect of the resistance on both groups are different. While Montanism dwindled and disappeared eventually, charismatics are gaining momentum and power. The future of the Pentecostal movement looks certain. However, one must not overlook the fact that Montanists thrived over centuries before its demise. Fourth, both groups made room for women to participate in their clergy. Fifth, the two groups had strong moral ethos, practiced fasting and ascetic living. Finally, they employed innovations in their service.

One major difference between the two movements is the use of their prophetic charisma. Adherents of Montanism used their prophetic charisma in an eschatological and apocalyptic manner. They spoke more about the second coming of Christ and how people should live and prepare for the Christ event. However, modern-day Pentecostals' use of prophetic charisma has shifted toward personal, family and governmental prophecies. Modern-day charismatic prophets mostly prophesy about everything, from election to childbearing, neglecting the eschatological and apocalyptic contents and parousia issues.

Finally, despite Montanism's description as a religious innovation, contemporary charismatic movements and Pentecostals appear to be more innovative than the Montanists. They use sophisticated media for the broadcast and spread of the gospel, urban-based mega-sized churches, dynamic styles of worship, motivational and prosperity-oriented messages and maintain a sense of internationalism, all of which attest to the various innovations being used to create space and to influence society.[59]

Conclusion

In conclusion, this paper sought to examine similarities and differences in the expression of Charisma between the Montanist movement and Pentecostals. One will agree that both movements have a lot in common. They share similar

---

59. Asamoah-Gyadu, *African Charismatics*, 31.

socioeconomic, political and religious backgrounds; they exhibit similar charismatic expressions with a strong emphasis on ascetic living, belief in the holy Scriptures, manifestations of the gifts, presence and abilities endowed by the Holy Spirit, acceptance of female counterparts into the clergy and the use of various innovations to facilitate the expressions of the movement.

There are also major differences, as noted above. The use of directive and predictive prophecy is more pronounced in Pentecostals, while Montanists emphasize more on apocalyptic and eschatological prophecies. The former tends to be more involved in the affairs of the people and their communities, helping with issues of the now, while the latter is concerned with the hereafter. Consequently, it is agreeable that Montanism has contributed greatly throughout the various epochs of the church by indicating, strongly, that the Holy Spirit is always working and doing greater things in each dispensation, as promised in Scripture.[60]

Furthermore, when members of the Christian community feel that the impact of the Spirit is not present, some members of the church find a way to bring the Spirit to the fore. This development demonstrates the Holy Spirit's importance in Christian expression, implying that the *ekklesia* on earth cannot exist without the Spirit's impactful role in Christian expression. In the light of this, however, whenever the Spirit is introduced, the traditional church, or the existing church, and its structures treat the "introductionist" or "pneumatologist" movements with hostility. Therefore, if the church wishes to avoid the rise of such pneumatological movements, the church must always try and keep the activities and roles of the Spirit central.

Bibliography

Adubofour, Samuel. "Evangelical Para Church Movement in Ghanaian Christianity: 1950 to Early 1990s." PhD Thesis, University of Edinburgh, 1994.

Anderson, Allan H. *Moya: The Spirit in an African Context*. Pretoria: University of South Africa, 1991.

Asamoah-Gyadu, J. Kwabena. *African Charismatics: Current Developments within Independent Indigenous Pentecostalism in Ghana*. Leiden: Brill, 2005.

———. *Contemporary Pentecostal Christianity: Interpretations from an African Context*. Oxford: Regnum, 2013.

---

60. Kim, "Is Montanism a Heretical Sect," 124.

———. *Sighs and Signs of the Spirit: Ghanaian Perspectives on Pentecostalism and Renewal in Africa*. Regnum Studies in Mission and Trends in African Christianity. Oxford: Regnum, 2015.

Baëta, Christian G. *Prophetism in Ghana: A Study of Some "Spiritual" Churches*. London: SCM, 1962.

Boamah, Kwaku. *Magic and Obstinacy of the Early Christians: Persecution and Martyrdoms in the Roman Empire*. Saarbrucken: Lambert Academic Publishing, 2012.

Cox, Harvey. *Fire from Heaven: The Rise of Pentecostal Spirituality and the Reshaping of Religion in the Twenty-First Century*. Reading: Addison-Wesley Publishing, 1995.

Denzey, Nicola. "What Did the Montanists Read?" *The Harvard Theological Review* 94, no. 4 (2001): 427–48.

Ekem, John D. K. *Priesthood in Context: A Study of Priesthood in Some Christian and Primal Communities of Ghana and Its Relevance for Mother-Tongue Biblical Interpretation*. Accra: Sonlife Press, 2009.

Gaffin, Richard B. *Perspectives on Pentecost*. Phillipsburg, NJ: Presbyterian and Reformed, 1979.

Gentry, Kenneth L., Jr. *The Charismatic Gift of Prophecy: A Reformed Analysis*. Lakeland: Whitefield Seminary Press, 1986.

Gifford, Paul. "The Prosperity Theology of David Oyedepo, Founder of Winners' Chapel." In *Pleasures of Plenty: Tracing Religio-Scapes of Prosperity Gospel in Africa and Beyond*, edited by Andreas Heuser, 83–100. Bern: Lang, 2015.

Gonzalez, Justo L. *A History of Christian Thought: From the Beginnings to the Council of Chalcedon*. Nashville: Abingdon Press, 1970.

Grayson, James H. "Montanism and the Empire of Mount Sion (시온산 제국): Lessons from the Early Church and the Early Korean Church." *Journal of Korean Religions* 2, no. 2 (2011): 83–110.

Hollenweger, Walter J. *Pentecostalism: Origins and Developments Worldwide*. Peabody: Hendrickson, 1997.

Kim, Lucien Jinkwang. "Is Montanism a Heretical Sect or Pentecostal Antecedent?" *Asian Journal Pentecostal Studies* 12, no. 1 (2009): 113–24.

Larbi, E. Kingsley. *Pentecostalism: The Eddies of Ghanaian Christianity*. Accra: CPCS, 2001.

Lynch, Joseph. *Early Christianity: A Brief History*. New York: Oxford University Press, 2010.

MacArthur, John. *The Charismatics: A Doctrinal Perspective*. Grand Rapids, MI: Zondervan, 1978.

Musurillo, Herbert. "The Martyrdom of Saints Perpetua and Felicitas." In *Acts of the Christian Martyrs*. Oxford: Clarendon, 1972.

Muzzey, David Saville. "Were the Spiritual Franciscans Montanist Heretics?" *The American Journal of Theology* 12, no. 4 (1908): 588–608.

Omenyo, Cephas N. *Pentecost outside Pentecostalism: A Study of the Development of Charismatic Renewal in the Mainline Churches in Ghana.* Zoetermeer: Boekencentrum, 2006.

Omenyo, Cephas N., and Abamfo O. Atiemo. "Claiming Religious Space: The Case of Neo-Prophetism in Ghana." *Ghana Bulletin of Theology* 1 (2006): 55–68.

Onyinah, Opoku. "Pentecostal Exorcism: Witchcraft and Demonology in Ghana." *Journal of Pentecostal Theology Supplement Series* 34 (2012): 1–349.

Oshitelu, G. A. *The African Fathers of The Early Church.* Ibadan: Sefer, 2002.

Reymond, Robert L. *What About Continuing Revelations and Miracles in the Presbyterian Church Today?* Phillipsburg: Presbyterian and Reformed, 1977.

Robeck, Cecil M. "Montanism and Present-Day 'Prophets.'" *Pneuma* 32, no. 4 (2010): 413–29.

Trevett, Christine. "Gender, Authority and Church History: A Case Study of Montanism." *Feminist Theology* 6, no. 17 (1998): 9–24.

———. "Montanism." In *The Early Christian World*, edited by Philip F. Esler, 929–51. London: Routledge, 2000.

3

Augustine's Articulation of the Holy Spirit

David K. Ngaruiya

Associate Professor, International Leadership University, Nairobi, Kenya

Abstract

Crucial to the work of God in the church and believers is the Holy Spirit. As the church in Africa grapples with unprecedented growth, the understanding of his person and work has split the church many times. In Kenya for example, a key factor in the split of mainline churches and the indigenous church was the understanding of the person and the work of the Holy Spirit. Even among the early church fathers, the articulation of the Holy Spirit had points of convergence but also notable points of divergence.

Augustine of Hippo, reputed as "the greatest and most influential of all the Christian Fathers" and no doubt a notable theologian over the centuries, is a case in point regarding pneumatology.[1] Augustine's articulation of the Holy Spirit is contested. On the one hand scholars such as Chad Gerber argue that Augustine's thinking regarding the Holy Spirit was not influenced by Plotinian thinking but rather Augustine used Plotinian thinking to enrich his thinking about the Holy Spirit. On the other hand, while noting some points of convergence, Du Roy argues that Augustine utilized reason in his early thinking regarding the Holy Spirit. Scholars such as Williams have found Augustine's

---

1. Philip Schaff, The *Nicene and Post-Nicene Fathers*, First Series, vol. 1 (Grand Rapids: Eerdmans 1979), v.

conflation of grace with Spirit problematic.² Nevertheless, Augustine's work has impacted the church and believers in many ways that are unparalleled and an exploration of his work is therefore a worthy undertaking.

This paper will therefore explore Augustinian articulation of the Holy Spirit in selected works including, but not limited to, *De Genesi ad litteram (The Literal Interpretation of Genesis)*, *Faith and the Creed*, the classic *Confessions*, his subsequent correction of errors published as *Retractions* and *De Trinitate*. In this exploration, the author argues that in Augustinian pneumatology, the Holy Spirit is divine, revealing the magnificence of the Father's love, active in creation and inspiring inerrant and united Scripture.

Key Words: Holy Spirit, Augustine, Trinity, creed, *Confessions*, *De Trinitate*.

Background

Augustine was born in 354 in Thagaste, an egregious town that is now "modern Souk Ahras," in present-day Algeria. Thagaste, administered from Carthage, was located about two hundred miles from the sea and, like many parts of the land, faced the reality of much brutality, near starvation and "bent backs" misery.³ His father was Patricius and his mother was Monica. It is evident from his writings that Augustine's mother was a dominant influence in his life. However, though couched in much economy of words in his writings, we know that Augustine possibly had two sisters and one brother, at least, named Navigius.

As Augustine narrates in *Confessions*, Patricius was a poor man who sacrificed all he could in order to educate his son.⁴ Thus, Augustine's world of growing up was one characterized by poverty, competitiveness and difficulties. In Augustine's time, Rome, although declining, had a great influence on Africa and many Africans like Augustine desired to have Roman education as a means to a better life. It was necessary for Augustine to be "civilized" and free in order to be fully a member of a Roman town. Augustine studied rhetoric and became a schoolmaster and later on a bishop. He was educated at Thagaste, then Madaura (a university town) and Carthage. While many are quick to embrace Augustinian philosophy, few take the time to understand his meteoric rise to

---

2. For detailed discussion see: Chad Tyler Gerber, *The Spirit of Augustine's Early Theology: Contextualizing Augustine's Pneumatology*, Ashgate Studies in Philosophy & Theology in Late Antiquity (Surrey; Burlington: Ashgate Publishing), 2012.

3. Brown, *Augustine of Hippo*, 8.

4. Augustine, *Confessions* 2.3.5.

prominence from the doldrums of immense poverty. The education aim of his time is brought out as "to learn the art of words, to acquire the eloquence that is essential to persuade men of your case, to unroll your opinions before them."[5] In this, Augustine is "guilty" as charged in his writings.

Like any scholar Augustine had limitations. For example, some allege that he had no knowledge of Greek. This is a misrepresentation of Augustine since he had knowledge of Greek that he acquired resulting from Latin translations even though it was not of great depth. He hardly had any knowledge of Hebrew and though he had extraordinary understanding of the Latin Bible, "he made many mistakes in exposition."[6] In style, Augustine would rather bear the criticism of grammarians than miss the opportunity to be understood by people.[7] Many of his writings are Psalm-like in tone. On one hand this shows the importance he placed on contextualization in the regard of being understood, and to some extent not paying attention to criticism on style on the other hand. Augustine may be described in many ways and not least of them as free thinking, rhetorician of the highest order, heretical in Manicheanism, skeptical, heathen philosopher before his conversion and a believing philosopher holding human reason highly but subservient to faith and theologian after his conversion.[8] Not unlike Paul, Augustine sought to become all things to all men.

The Holy Spirit and Creation in the Genesis Account

In his commentary *De Genesi ad litteram* Augustine brings out the divinity of the Holy Spirit and the third person of the Trinity. Augustine's interpretation of creation is two-phased. The first phase is *terra informis* comprising unsolidified substance that is shapeless consisting of *coelum et terra*, that is heaven and earth, after which came *incomposita et abbysus*, and water. In the second phase, "the substance is shaped" and becomes *materia informis*, and becomes a perfect creation. According to Augustine, it is the Holy Spirit – who Augustine calls Holy Spirit Creator – who forms *materia informis* to specific shapes.[9] Considering that in AD 325 the divinity of the Holy Spirit was under

---

5. Augustine, *Confessions* 1.16.26. See also Brown, 24.
6. Schaff, *Nicene and Post-Nicene Fathers*, First Series, 9.
7. Schaff, 11.
8. Schaff.
9. Berkovic, "'Merahefet,'" 171–83.

intense arguments by some, such as Bishop Marcedonius, it is noteworthy that Augustine had settled on the divinity of the Holy Spirit.[10]

That the Spirit of God is an active person and independent of creation is clear from Augustine's statement that "Thy good Spirit was borne over the waters, not borne up by them as if he rested upon them. For those in whom Thy good Spirit is said to rest He causes to rest in Himself."[11] It is also noteworthy that Augustine refers to the Spirit of God as good to express his character and distinguish him from other spirits. Moreover, Augustine recognizes that he, the good Spirit, gives rest. To Augustine, the divinity of the Holy Spirit is evident from the Genesis account. Not only was the Holy Spirit present in creation but he is also active in all that God created.

The Holy Spirit in the *Confessions* of St. Augustine

Augustine's connection of rest with the Holy Spirit is significant. On this theme of rest, Augustine famously declared that "Thou hast formed us for Thyself and our hearts are restless till they find rest in Thee."[12] This "confession" of Augustine is notable for a man who sought fulfillment from worldly pleasures, philosophy, cults and squandering of resources, among other things.

Augustine, in his *Confessions*, asserts

> Behold now, the Trinity appears unto me in an enigma, which Thou, O my God, art, since Thou, O Father, in the beginning of our wisdom.... And under the name of God, I now held the Father, who made these things; and under the name of the Beginning, the Son, in whom He made these things; and believing as I did that my God was the Trinity, I sought further in His holy words, and behold, Thy Spirit was borne over the waters. Behold, the Trinity, O my God, Father, Son and Holy Ghost – the Creator of all creation.[13]

Augustine's conceptualization of the Trinity, of which the Holy Spirit is a part, was an enigma, a translation from Latin conveying a sense of mystery and paradox. To both Catholics and Protestants, the Holy Trinity is a point of concurrence. This point of concurrence from Augustine who upheld a

---

10. Berkovic, 174.
11. Augustine, *Confessions*, 13.4.5.
12. Augustine, *Confessions*, 1.1.1.
13. Augustine, *Confessions*, 13.5.6 (NPNF 1/1:191).

principle of coercing and persecuting schismatics and heretics by "a false exegesis" of Luke 14:23 to read "compel them to come in," and which led to much unnecessary suffering and poor witness of the Christian faith, cannot be understated.[14]

Although distinctly a person, the Holy Spirit is inseparable from the Trinity. Besides these, the doctrine of the Holy Trinity in which the Holy Spirit is person to the order Father, Son and Holy Spirit is to Augustine a clear matter having been derived not from conjecture but from Scripture.

Faith and Creeds

It is important to keep in mind the context of the *Faith and the Creed* in regard to Augustine's understanding of the Holy Spirit. In AD 393, the African church held a plenary council.[15] Aurelius, having become Bishop of Carthage in 390 was on good terms and of one mind with Augustine that the African church needed some reform. From their correspondence with one another, it seems like Augustine had made suggestions regarding holding a council to address reforms in the African church. In 391 Aurelius had in writing communicated to Augustine about the reform council and extended an invitation to Augustine to address the council. In this discourse, Augustine exposits articles of the Creed to defend its doctrine against critics among them – philosophers, heretics including Arians, Sabellians, Manichees and Apollinarians, as well as Donatists and Novatianists both of whom were schismatics. This was the context in which Augustine lays the understanding of the person and work of the Holy Spirit.

Augustine is consistent in articulation of the Holy Spirit as divine. For Augustine, "The Holy Spirit is not by nature less than the Father or Son, but is, if I may say so consubstantial and co-eternal with them" and at the same time distinct from the Father and the Son.[16] Augustine draws this Trinitarian understanding from Deuteronomy 6:4. He further anticipates and preempts the notion that since Christians worship a Trinitarian God and they cannot be charged of worshipping three gods since it is said of the Trinity that "For of him and through him and to him are all things" according to Romans 11:36. It is significant to note that Augustine expresses this in the context of his article *Faith and the Creed*, one of his earlier writings whose context is mentioned above and in defense of the Christian faith.

---

14. Schaff, *Nicene and Post-Nicene Fathers*, 17.
15. Burleigh, *Augustine*, 351.
16. Burleigh, *Augustine*, 361–62.

Another doctrine that Augustine defends against critics is the virgin birth in which the Holy Spirit plays a very prominent role. According to Augustine, the gift of God that is the Holy Spirit reveals the humility of God. This humility is expressed through God inhabiting the body of Mary, a virgin in whom God takes upon himself whole human nature and leaving Mary's body pure and whole having been born of it.[17] This defense of the incarnation was aimed to not only affirm the church's position on this matter but also to answer critics who were attacking this doctrine, some to the extent of denying Mary as the mother of Jesus. Augustine further defends the virgin birth by clarifying that though Jesus did not have a divine mother, he was nonetheless born of a human mother.[18] Whether Augustine is relating the Holy Spirit to the Trinity or the virgin birth, he maintains that the Holy Spirit is divine.

While some affirm Augustine's thinking of the Holy Spirit as "love" and "gift," some theologians object to the use of this term even though "love" and "gift" have been a critical linchpin in many centuries of Western theologians, whether Catholic or Protestant. According to Ephraim Radner, to name the Spirit as "love" and "gift" is "a bad idea" because it creates "within the Western tradition a principle of pneumatic abstraction, capable in theory of being decoupled from Christian particularities."[19] Augustine's view of the Holy Spirit perceiving him as *vinculum caritas*, which is divine love between Son and Father, is sometimes criticized as devaluing the Holy Spirit's personhood.

Confessions of St. Augustine

There is to Augustine a puzzle as to why the Holy Spirit is preceded by a mention of heaven, unformed earth and darkness over the deep rather than the precedence of the Holy Spirit in the creation account. Augustine states:

> But why, O truth-speaking Light? To you I lift up my heart, let it not teach me worthless things. Disperse it shadows and tell me I pray, by that love which is our mother, the reason why Your Scripture at long last referred to your Spirit, but only after the reference to heaven, to the invisible and unformed earth, and the darkness over the abyss? Was it because it was appropriate that he should first be shown to us as "moving over"? If so, this couldn't

---

17. Burleigh, 358.
18. Burleigh, 358.
19. Radner, "Holy Spirit and Unity," 209.

have been said unless something had already been mentioned over which Your Spirit could be understood as "moving." Didn't He move over the Father and the Son? He couldn't properly be said to be "moving over" if He were moving over nothing. Thus, what He was "moving over" had to be identified before He could then be mentioned. Nevertheless, why wasn't it fitting that He be introduced in some other way than in this context of "moving over"?[20]

In this puzzle, one may decipher that Augustine would have anticipated the Holy Spirit, who was involved in creation would be mentioned before the mentioning of heaven, earth and darkness. After all, the Holy Spirit is indispensable in the creation act as part of the Holy Trinity.

Augustine expresses the magnificence of God's love poured out by his Spirit who is not just a gift to man.[21] In addition, the Holy Spirit's sanctity elevates man by "love of release from anxiety" as opposed to the filthiness of the human soul that is drawn downward by worldly love.[22] It should be a mystery that God's Holy Spirit comes down to a filthy soul but the accompaniment of God's love unravels that mystery. Thus by the Spirit of God, man is rescued in love by God. What a mystery not only to Augustine but to all who marvel at God's love and rescue of a filthy soul, which is true of every human being. Further to this, it is he, the Holy Spirit, who reconciles man to God and he is therefore the love of God.[23] This biblical and theological truth of the Holy Spirit being the "love of God" is not a very common expression among Christians.

Should it be surprising that Augustine marvels at God's love? Perhaps not! After all, Augustine had fathomed the depth of depravity to which man without God was sunk. Even more so, the destiny of a sinning soul could only be contemplated in the deepest misery that humans can fathom. Yet, through the "love of release" man could contemplate a destiny of bliss before his maker and of which the Holy Spirit is party. Thus, the Holy Spirit expresses the magnificence of the Father's love.

---

20. Augustine, *Confessions*, 387. Trans. Gill.
21. Augustine, *Confessions* 13.7.8.
22. Augustine, *Confessions*, 388. Trans. Gill.
23. Burleigh, *Augustine*, 364.

Augustine's Hermeneutic

Augustine's reverence of the Holy Spirit shines through his penetrating questions posed not to himself but to God the Father. As would be the case in interrogating Augustine's understanding of Scripture, it is critical to look at Augustine's hermeneutic.

According to Augustine, like other church fathers, Scripture is Holy Spirit-inspired in whole and as such without contradiction. Further, Scripture is inerrant and unified. As such, Scripture possesses for a reader various levels inviting different interpretations of a particular text depending on whether one reads them in a literal or spiritual sense. While three or four levels of Scripture were identified by many church fathers, Augustine in at least two texts identifies four levels: "the etiological, the historical, the anagogical and the allegorical."[24]

This four way of interpreting Scripture is called the "quadriga" and lasted from the fourth to the sixteenth century. This approach to Scripture, which would later form the battleground of the Reformers who objected to it, was taught through employing a well-known jingle:

> The letter shows us what God and our Fathers did
> The allegory shows us where our faith is hid;
> The moral meaning gives us rules of daily life;
> The anagogy shows us where we end our strife.[25]

Augustine's book *On Christian Doctrine* based on this method became "the basic hermeneutical" reference model of the Middle Ages.[26] One may also consider Augustine's earlier work on Genesis where he took the seven days of creation to be understood as "7 stages of the Christian life."[27]

Augustine's understanding of inspired Scripture however needed to relate to the authority of the church. His perspective was, "ego vero Evangelio non crederem, nisi me catholicae Ecclesiae commoveret auctoritas" ("I will not truly believe the Gospel if the Catholic Church does not guarantee its authority for me"), an extreme position inferring the superiority of the church vis-à-vis the canon of Scripture.[28] Furthermore, in coming to terms with canonical

---

24. Harrison, "Augustine," 77.
25. McQuilkin, *Understanding and Applying the Bible*, 39.
26. Muller, *Dictionary of Latin and Greek*, 254.
27. Augustine, *De Genesis contra Manichaeos* 1.12.35–1.25.43. See also Augustine of Hippo, "On Christian Doctrine," in *St. Augustin's City of God and Christian Doctrine*, ed. Philip Schaff, trans. J. F. Shaw, vol. 2, A Select Library of the Nicene and Post-Nicene Fathers of the Christian Church, First Series (Buffalo, NY: Christian Literature Company, 1887), 538.
28. Schnabel, "History, Theology and the Biblical Canon," 16.

Scripture, Catholicism, it must be noted, embraces extra-canonical books. In Augustinian thought, Scripture was Holy-Spirit inspired without contradiction, inerrant and united.

Critiques of Augustine on the Holy Spirit

While many have been influenced and inspired by Augustinian understanding of the Holy Spirit, others have found this understanding problematic. Not least among them is Norman Williams. Williams puts his criticism of Augustine as follows:

> If Augustine had frankly equated sanctifying grace with the work of the Holy Spirit his thought would have been at least continuous with that of St. Paul; and, as terminology is merely a matter of convenience, the slight perversion of the Pauline term kindness to denote God's kind and healing power which is the Third Person of His Triune Being would have been pardonable and indeed useful, if care had been taken to guard against the tendency to hypostatize "grace" as an entity other than Spirit.[29]

This Augustinian thinking is seen as a perversion "view of God's creative and redemptive relationship with mankind."[30] While such criticisms have their place, they do not diminish the influence that Augustine yields in his theology of the Holy Spirit. While Williams may find Augustine to be at odds with Paul, Augustine's work on the Holy Spirit continues to influence many Christians.

De Trinitate

Many scholars are of the opinion that Augustine's *De Trinitate* focuses on the Trinity. While not denying that *De Trinitate* seeks to answer questions on the Holy Trinity, it is plausible to think of *De Trinitate* as offering teaching that is largely pneumatological, while not neglecting matters of the Holy Trinity.[31] "The Holy Spirit . . . too is God and not a creature. And, if He is not a creature, then He is not only God . . . but also true God; therefore absolutely equal to the Father and the Son, and consubstantial and co-eternal in the oneness of

---

    29. N. P. Williams *The Grace of God* (Longmans, Green and Co. 1930), 25. See also David C. Shipley, "Grace and Spirit in the Augustinian Tradition" in *Anglican Theological Review*, 37 no. 4 Oct 1955: 241–249.
    30. Ibid.
    31. Awad, "Another Puzzle," 1.

the three."³² This preceding statement from *De Trinitate* by Augustine is an indicator of the Holy Spirit as an important theme in this book. *De Trinitate* is thus a rich source of understanding Augustinian pneumatology.

In considering *De Trinitate*, Awad opines that with a disjuncture this opens a door of possibility that Augustine could have been aiming to write an additional account of Holy Spirit doctrine, which he already subscribed to, or he could have been aiming at contributing new understandings regarding this neglected aspect of doctrine in the church. This could further suggest that Augustine's formulation of the Holy Trinity doctrine carried much weight in teaching about the Holy Spirit.³³

This weight is not without evidence. Augustine states, "Another puzzle [which worries people] is in what manner the Holy Spirit is in the three, being begotten neither by Father nor Son nor both of them, while being the Spirit both of the Father and the Son."³⁴ Thus the theme of the Holy Spirit is foremost in Augustine's mind. As a matter of fact, it is a major matter that he seeks to address in *De Trinitate*.

Augustine's consideration regarding the "how" and "when" of the revelation of the Holy Trinity brings the importance of the Holy Spirit to the fore.³⁵ The New Testament is the source of Augustine's understanding of this revelation. It is the mission of the Son as well as the mission of the Holy Spirit that lay out the understanding of the Holy Trinity's revelation, as one can gather from the New Testament. Augustine states:

> As being born means for the Son being from the Father, so being sent means for the Son his being known to be from the Father. And as being the gift of God means for the Holy Spirit proceeding from the Father, so being sent means for the Holy Spirit his being known to proceed from the Father.³⁶

Thus the role of the Holy Spirit in the revelation of the Holy Trinity is critical in Augustinian thought.

According to Augustine, the Holy Spirit is not subordinate to the Father or the Son. Instead, he is the love between them. In this complex argument, Augustine states, "when we say, therefore, 'the gift of the giver' and 'the giver of

---

32. Augustine, *On the Trinity*, 1.2.13.
33. Augustine.
34. Awad, "Another Puzzle," 4.
35. Augustine, "Sermons," 282.
36. Augustine, *On the Trinity*, 4.20.29.

the gift,' we speak in both cases relatively in reciprocal reference."[37] Although this statement sparks a lot of debate, is it clear from Augustinian thinking that the Holy Spirit is just as prominent as the Father and the Son? This is posed as a question deliberately, recognizing that this can be very controversial in orthodoxy. To Augustine, it should be remembered that "with reference to creation, Father, Son and Holy Spirit are one origin, just as they are one Creator and one Lord"[38] and thus he cannot be accused of downplaying the Holy Spirit in relation to the Father and Son. Once again, one need not surmise the importance and prominence of the Holy Spirit in Augustinian thought for Augustine provides much data on this perspective.

It should be noted that in as much as one may argue that Augustine at no time downplays the person of the Holy Spirit, criticism abounds regarding his pneumatology. Gunton and Moltmann are examples in this criticism. According to Gunton, to conceive the Holy Spirit as gift and love is problematic.[39] Moltmann in his criticism of Augustine's "love" pneumatology is one in which the Godhead is reduced to a duality.[40] Furthermore, "in *filioque*, or the 'reduction' of the Holy Spirit to '*donum*' and especially '*caritas*' between the Father and Son. These emphases appear not only to de-emphasize the Spirit's personal nature, but also to subordinate the Third Person in the face of the First and Second Persons."[41] Interestingly, Augustine in *De Trinitate* warns against such misunderstanding and many scholars consider such criticisms as being based on ignorance of Augustine's work in its primary state.[42] Kuehn's work reflects a defense of Augustine.

In *De Trinitate*, Augustine asserts

> [Christ] gives his reason for saying, *[the Spirit] will receive of mine*; namely, *All that the Father has is mine; that is why I said he will receive of mine*. And so we are left to understand that the Holy Spirit has [all that the Father has] just like the Son.[43]

---

37. Phillip Schaff, *Nicene and Post-Nicene Fathers*, First Series, vol. 3 (Grand Rapids, MI: Christian Ethereal Library), 188.
38. Awad, "Another Puzzle," 13.
39. Ormerod, "Augustine and the Trinity," 17–32.
40. Moltmann, *The Trinity and the Kingdom*, 16, 143.
41. Kuehn, "Johanine Logic of Augustine's Trinity," 576.
42. Ayres, *Nicaea and Its Legacy*, 364.
43. Kuehn, 578.

Though some scholars may criticize Augustine his understanding of the Holy Spirit, at no time does Augustine in his writings deny that the Holy Spirit is divine and Third member of the Holy Trinity.

The Holy Spirit in "A Treatise on the Spirit and the Letter"

In this work, Augustine refers to the Holy Spirit of God as the "finger of God."[44] In a sermon, Augustine with much clarity explains "the finger of God." Based on Luke 11:20 and Mathew 12:28, Augustine here uses "Scripture to interpret Scripture" and states that "the Holy Spirit is the finger of God." To Augustine, the question as to why the Spirit is called the "finger of God" is important and to this Augustine asserts that "It's because the apostles received a division of gifts (1 Cor 12:4) through the Holy Spirit and the division of the hand is apparent in fingers; with them one counts and distributes."[45]

The courage and hope wrought by the "finger of God" from Augustine is expressed at what some may consider the height of faith in Christian suffering. In Augustine's sermon, to be filled with "the finger of God" is to be intoxicated by him such that nothing in the world enthralls us more, just as the martyrs were to the extent while they faced such painful death. In that state, the martyrs:

> forgot children and wives, and parents throwing dust on their hands, and their mothers pulling their breasts to reproach them with the milk they had sucked, and refusing to eat, they forgot everything, didn't even recognize their own people. Why be surprised even when a martyr doesn't recognize his own people? The man's drunk. But what he drunk on? On charity. And where is he getting charity from? From the finger of God, from the Holy Spirit, from the one who came at Pentecost.[46]

Augustinian pneumatology thus recognizes that though suffering is a reality of our world even for the saints, the Holy Spirit is a resource in coping with Christian suffering.

---

44. "On the Spirit and the Letter," I, 28, XVI (See page 95 of *Nicene and Post-Nicene Fathers*, First Series, vol. 5).

45. Augustine, "Sermons," 307.

46. Augustine, 309.

Relevance of Augustinian Pneumatology in Contemporary Africa

This section will explore relevance of Augustinian pneumatology to the contemporary African church. It will cover this relevance on matters of doctrine, preaching, theology, courage and hope.

Doctrine

Augustine engaged his opponents vigorously on matters of doctrine. An example of this is his use of rhetoric about the Holy Spirit and *"gratia"* as a theme with his opponents who were no less than his enemies. This was a battle that Augustine fought magnanimously, intense as it was. African Christianity in all its multicolor gown has much conflict within it on doctrine, particularly on that of the Holy Spirit. Furthermore, African theologians themselves have dealt with the doctrine of Holy Spirit extensively and in context.[47] Like Augustine, African theologians must keep rising to the occasion by engaging errant doctrine even when their churches remain orthodox. While one may commend the All-Africa Conference of Churches for bringing churches together to discuss doctrine among other things, the mushrooming of many cults on the continent, sometimes occasioned by the rise of diverse forms of church governance, calls theologians to constantly address this matter of Holy Spirit doctrine. The African indigenous church, of which the Spirit-type church is part, is a rich source of data on understanding pneumatology that in turn would contribute much to the doctrine of the Holy Spirit.

Preaching

To Augustine, the pulpit was the platform of Christian ministry. The power of sermons, good or bad, is undeniable. As historians and classical scholars have started noting the cultural and historical impact of Christian sermons bold assertions are being made, ". . . the sermon was Christianity's foremost contribution to ancient culture, representing 'nothing less than a revolution in the politics of literary production, a democratization theorized, in fact by Augustine himself.'"[48]

That Holy Spirit-enabled preaching is essential in the African church is undeniable. Like Augustine, the African church must confront errant doctrine through Spirit-led preaching. In the wake of prosperity gospel, gospel of

---

47. Anderson, *Moya*, 6.
48. Ando, "Christian Literature," 405.

poverty and cult churches where personalities are worshipped and adored for their financially dispensed anointing, blessing and healing, the contemporary African church must hold firmly to solid Bible-based preaching.

Hermeneutics

Augustine approached Scripture as Spirit-inspired and handled the biblical text as sacred. His four way of interpreting Scripture known as the "quadriga," with its strengths and weaknesses, was applied with vigor. In recent years, while holding Scripture to be sacred, some African theologians have formulated hermeneutical tools in treatment of sacred Scripture. A recent example of this is *African Hermeneutics* in which African culture and "worldview" are important influences and considerations in interpreting sacred Scripture contextually.[49] As a dynamic field with much Christian heritage from which to draw, hermeneutics is key not only in how we are to approach Scripture but also the way we let the Spirit of God methodically help us grasp truth. In other words, African Christian theologians and Christian intellectuals in each generation should seek to be grounded in relevant hermeneutics.

Courage and Hope

African Christianity, thriving as it may be, is also surrounded by many challenges that require courage and hope. There are challenges of institutionalized poverty where in a continent endowed with much and rare mineral wealth that drives the world of technology, where mortality rates remain some of the highest in the world and where governance is chaotic, to say the least, in independence but with little democratic structures, such hope and courage is required.

The assertions and imagery that Augustine uses of martyrdom are freeing in reminding believers to take up their daily cross and to march their walk of faith with hope and courage since the "finger of God" and his attendant grace is upon them.

Conclusion

The person and work of the Holy Spirit loom large in Augustinian pneumatology. In the creation account, the "Holy Spirit Creator" forms *materia informis* to specific shapes thus playing a prominent role in creation. In the *Faith and the*

---

49. Mburu, *African Hermeneutics*, x.

Creed discourse, Augustine defends doctrine against critics not least among them being philosophers and Donatists. It is in the context of confronting heresy that Augustine expresses and expounds his understanding of the Holy Spirit. In his *Confessions* the magnificence of God's love comes by the person of the Holy Spirit. In *De Trinitate* pneumatology is a prominent theme. Though Augustine has critiques on salient matters of pneumatology, his teachings continue to impact the church and inspire many individual Christians in many areas such as doctrine, preaching, hermeneutics as well as courage and hope in the midst of suffering. From these we conclude that in Augustinian pneumatology, the Holy Spirit is divine revealing the magnificence of the Father's love, active in creation and inspired, inerrant and united Scripture.

Bibliography

Anderson, Allan H. *Moya: The Holy Spirit in an African Context*. Pretoria: University of South Africa, 1991.

Ando, Clifford. "Christian Literature." In *Edinburgh Companion to Ancient Greece and Rome*, edited by Edward Bispham, Thomas Harrison, and Brian A. Sparkes, 402–6. Edinburgh: Edinburgh University Press, 2006.

Augustine. *Confessions: Saint Augustine*, trans. Tom Gill. Gainesville, FL: Bridge-Logos, 2003.

———, *Contra Ep. Man.*, cap. 5 (Migne PL 42, 176).

———. "Sermons." In *The Works of Saint Augustine: A Translation for the 21st Century*, translated by Edmund Hill. Brooklyn: New City Press, 1993.

Awad, Najeeb. "'Another Puzzle Is . . . the Holy': *De Trinitate* as Augustine's Pneumatology." *Scottish Journal of Theology* 65, no. 1 (2012): 1–16.

Ayres, Lewis. *Nicaea and Its Legacy: An Approach to Fourth Century Trinitarian Theology*. Oxford: Oxford University Press, 2006.

Berkovic, Danijel. "'Merahefet' (Genesis 1:2) The Dynamics of the Spirit in the Old Testament." *Kairos* 1, no. 2 (2007): 171–83.

Brown, Peter. *Augustine of Hippo: A Biography*. Berkeley: University of California Press, 2000.

Burleigh, J. H. S., ed. *Augustine: Earlier Writings*. Philadelphia: Westminster, 1979.

Dreyfus, Francois. "L'Actualisation De L'écriture: I. - Du Texte A La Vie." *Revue Biblique* 86, no. 1 (1979): 5–58.

Gerber, Chad Tyler. *The Spirit of Augustine's Early Theology: Contextualizing Augustine's Pneumatology*. Ashgate Studies in Philosophy & Theology in Late Antiquity. Surrey; Burlington: Ashgate Publishing, 2012.

Grabowski, Stanislaus J. "Spiritus Dei in Genesis 1:2 According to St. Augustine." *Catholic Biblical Quarterly* 10, no. 1 (1948): 13–28.

Harrison, Carol. "Augustine." In *Dictionary for Theological Interpretation of the Bible*, edited by Kevin J. Van Hoozer, 76–78. Grand Rapids: Baker Academic, 2006.

Kuehn, Evan F. "The Johannine Logic of Augustine's Trinity: A Dogmatic Sketch." *Theological Studies* 68, no. 3 (2007): 572–94.

Mburu, Elizabeth. *African Hermeneutics*. Carlisle, UK: HippoBooks, 2019.

McQuilkin, Robertson. *Understanding and Applying the Bible*. Chicago, IL: Moody Press, 1992.

Moltmann, Jurgen. *The Trinity and the Kingdom*. San Francisco: Harper & Row, 1981.

Muller, Richard A. *Dictionary of Latin and Greek Theological Terms: Drawn Principally from Protestant Scholastic Theology*. Grand Rapids: Baker Books, 2006.

Ormerod, Neil. "Augustine and the Trinity: Whose Crisis?" *Pacifica* 16, no. 1 (2003): 17–32.

Ortlund, Gavin. "Did Augustine Read Genesis 1 Literally?" *Sapientia*, Carl F. H. Henry Center for Theological Understanding, 4 September 2017. Available online, https://henrycenter.tiu.edu/2017/09/did-augustine-read-genesis-1-literally/.

Radner, Ephraim. "The Holy Spirit and Unity: Getting Out of the Way of Christ." *International Journal of Systematic Theology* 16, no. 2 (2014): 207–20.

Sanlon, Peter. *Augustine's Theology of Preaching*. Minneapolis: Fortress Press, 2014.

Schaff, Philip. *Nicene and Post-Nicene Fathers*, First Series. Grand Rapids: Eerdmans, 1979.

Schnabel, Eckhard. "History, Theology and the Biblical Canon: An Introduction to Basic Issues." *Themelios* 20, no. 2 (1995): 16–24.

Shipley, David C. "Grace and Spirit in the Augustinian Tradition." *Anglican Theological Review* 37, no. 4 Oct 1955: 241–49.

4

Pneumatology and Mission of the Church in Postmodern Africa

The Holy Spirit in Trinitarian Theology as Panacea

John Michael Kiboi
Senior Lecturer, St. Paul's University, Limuru, Kenya

Abstract

The Old Testament word for Spirit, *ruach* that was translated into Greek as *pneuma*, literally means wind. The Greek notion of *pneuma* relates to *dunamis*, a word that refers to power and conveys forcefulness. Some neo-Pentecostal churches and churches of the Holy Spirit have adopted this notion and this has consequently resulted in the perception of the Holy Spirit as an impersonal force from God. This notion has then further led the neo-Pentecostal churches and the churches of the Holy Spirit to regard the work of the Holy Spirit as the work of an impersonal force and not God. This has also led to the belief that to be sure that one is indwelt by this impersonal force the believer should manifest its gifts, for example speaking in tongues. Since the mainline churches do not exhibit these signs, they have been accused of lacking the Holy Spirit. This accusation causes anxiety among the members of the mainline churches as they doubt their own salvation. However, in self-defense, the mainline churches on their part accuse the neo-Pentecostals of reducing the Spirit of God to mere commodity of trade. Such accusations and counter-accusations undermine the unity of the church as the body of Christ. In the context of a postmodern church, epistemological questions are inevitable: Is speaking in tongues the only mark of being indwelt by the Holy Spirit? How do I know that the tongues are genuine and not fake? Neo-Pentecostal claims and postmodern doubts are both a result of poor knowledge of pneumatology. Poor knowledge of this doctrine is because in the formative years of the church pneumatology was the least discussed doctrine. It wasn't until the eighteenth and nineteenth centuries in general, when Pentecostal churches claimed that speaking in tongues was evidence of being indwelt by the power of the Holy Spirit, that this doctrine was readily discussed. This chapter employs ontological-existentialism to argue that an explication of pneumatology from a Trinitarian point will illuminate the doctrine of the Holy Spirit and this will clear the misconceptions and resolve the postmodern epistemological doubt on the work of the Holy Spirit.

Key words: pneumatology, mission, Trinitarian pneumatology, postmodernity, skepticism, heresies, ontological-existential, neo-Pentecostalism

Introduction

Nyabwari and Kagema state that churches of the Holy Spirit and neo-Pentecostal churches understand the person of the Holy Spirit as an impersonal force of God.[1] Neo-Pentecostal churches teach that when this impersonal force indwells a believer, the believer manifests evidence of its indwelling through speaking in tongues,[2] failure of which is evidence that the believer did not receive the Spirit. Since many of the mainline churches do not speak in tongues, they have been accused of not possessing this power of God. This accusation causes anxiety among the members of the mainline churches as they doubt their own salvation. However, in self-defense, the mainline churches on their part accuse the neo-Pentecostals of reducing the Spirit of God to mere commodity of trade. They pose the question, is it (or isn't it) possible for some people to fake tongues? These accusations divide the body of Christ.

In the context of postmodernity, epistemological questions on the problem of religious knowledge arise: Is it possible to know anything? How can one know that they know? A nexus to the epistemological question is the problem of theological language – what language would one use to explain their religious experience? These questions aggravate postmodern skeptical

---

1. Nyabwari and Kagema, "Charismatic Pentecostal Churches," 27–33.
2. Anderson, et al., *Studying Global Pentecostalism*, 167.

doubt and relativism, which makes preaching the work and manifestation of the Holy Spirit in a postmodern epoch difficult.

This chapter hypothesizes that if the doctrine of the Holy Spirit is explained from a Trinitarian view point it can assist in addressing misconceptions about the Holy Spirit's personhood. It will also correct the postmodern skepticism on the work of the Holy Spirit in a believer, for we cannot separate the person and the work of the Holy Spirit. It will also correct the neo-Pentecostal claim that speaking in tongues is the sure evidence of being indwelt by the Holy Spirit. Thus, this article proposes that approaches toward pneumatology should be ontological-existential rather than existential-ontological.

Pneumatology in History

A survey of the doctrine of pneumatology in its historical contexts will help us demonstrate that pneumatological heresies were a result of limited knowledge on the person of the Holy Spirit. However, in such a short paper, it is not possible to analyze every form this doctrine may have taken. For this reason, this paper will deal with major heresies that attacked the person of the Holy Spirit.

Misconception of the Holy Spirit in the History of the Church

Anomoean Pneumatolgy

One of the earliest misconceptions of the person of the Holy Spirit reported is the Anomoean[3] heresy in the fourth century. The Anomoean "began from the idea that God was *per se* ingenerate essence . . . and argued that the Son was unlike (*anomoios*) the Father in substance."[4] Based on this principle, they held that the Spirit was second in rank of created beings after the Son.[5] They thus denied the deity of the Holy Spirit.

Pneumatomachianism

Pneumatomachians, also known as Spirit-fighters, or Macedonianism (after former bishop of Constantinople named Macedonius, a semi-Arianist), did

---

3. Anomoeans were followers of Eunomius in the fourth century.
4. G. A. Keith, "Arianism" in Ferguson, Wright, and Packer, *New Dictionary of Theology*, 43. Also see David F. Wright, "Councils and Creeds" in *A Lion Handbook*, 172.
5. Keith, "Arianism," 43.

not find scriptural support for the divinity of the Holy Spirit.[6] They taught that the Holy Spirit was a creature who was subordinate to God the Father and the Son and had been created to serve as a servant of the two persons of the Godhead.[7]

The fathers at the council of Constantinople in 381 sought to correct and clarify that the Holy Spirit was consubstantial (*homoousious*) with the other persons of the Godhead. They wrote, "we believe in the Holy Spirit, the Lord and Giver of Life, who proceeds from the Father and the Son. With the Father and the Son he is worshipped and glorified. He has spoken through the Prophets."[8]

Tropici

Tropici (also spelled *tropicii*) was a fourth-century sect whose interpretation of Scripture took a position that the Spirit was not divine.[9] Reading Zechariah 1:9 alongside Hebrews 1:14, which states, "Are not all angels spirits in the divine service, sent to serve for the sake of those who are to inherit salvation?,"[10] and Amos 4:13, "For lo, the one who forms the mountains, creates the wind [*ruach*] . . .," they regarded the spirit as one of the highest ranking angels and therefore a creature of God, created for divine service. They therefore, rejected the Nicaean testimony of affirming that the Spirit was *homouousios* with the Father and the Son and instead regarded the Spirit as of different essence (*heteroousios*) from the Father and the Son.[11]

Athanasius wrote to refute the *tropici* interpretation and teachings regarding the person of the Holy Spirit. In his repudiation, he affirmed the divinity and the co-substantiality of the Holy Spirit with the Father and the Son. Using Scriptures he demonstrated that the Spirit shared the nature with the other persons of the Holy Trinity. His argument was that scriptures taught that the Holy Spirit received honor and worship just like the other two persons of the Godhead and therefore, the Holy Spirit was also God.

---

6. Keith, "Arianism," 43.
7. "What Was the Pneumatomachian Heresy," *GotQuestions*, https://www.gotquestions.org/Pneumatomachian-Macedonianism.html.
8. Anglican Church of Kenya, *Our Modern Services*, 118–19.
9. Davis, "Importance of Athanasius," 95.
10. Scripture references in this chapter are taken from NRSV unless otherwise indicated.
11. Davis, 95.

Filioque Controversy

According to the pneumatology of the Nicene Council, the Spirit proceeds from the Father through the Son. This position was altered during the sixth century at the Council of Toledo (589). The council had interpreted John 15:26 as implying double procession. The text reads, "When the Advocate comes, whom I will send to you from the Father, the Spirit of truth who comes from the Father, he will testify on my behalf." The council read, "whom I will send from the Father" as a procession from the Son and "the Spirit of truth who comes from the Father" as another procession.

However, Ferguson observes that "It is natural to suppose that the double sending of the Spirit reflects, and so reveals, a double procession in the divine life-pattern, but Scripture speaks only of the former, leaving the latter totally opaque to us in fact, however much it is argued over."[12] It is this addition of the *filioque* (*and* the Son) in the original clause that caused the great schism of 1054.

Manifestations of Pneumatological Heresies in neo-Pentecostalism

Neo-Pentecostalism is the latest wave of general Pentecostal movements. This is a wave of charismatic churches that has become a significant phenomenon on the African continent since 1970 and 1980s.[13] Joe Kayo, David Kimani, Bethel Mission and Margret Wangari were the earliest practitioners of neo-Pentecostalism in Kenya.[14] Parsitau and Mwaura corroborate Allan Anderson and Ogbu Kalu and posit that these churches emphasize healing, deliverance and the gospel of prosperity.[15]

These movements lay emphasis on high-spirited praise and the exercise of various gifts by the congregation under the influence of the Holy Spirit. This emphasis has posed a challenge in their understanding of the person of the Holy Spirit. It appears that the notion of the Holy Spirit among these groups has been mutating from one strand to the other.

---

12. J. I. Packer, "Holy Spirit" in Ferguson, Wright, and Packer, *New Dictionary of Theology*, 318.
13. Parsitau and Mwaura, "God in the City," 1–2.
14. Nyabwari and Kagema, "Charismatic Pentecostal Churches," 1.
15. Parsitau and Mwaura, "God in the City," 6.

These neo-Pentecostal churches define the Holy Spirit as divine impersonal force.[16] Nyabwari observes that "the key focus in neo-Pentecostalism is the working of Holy Spirit who has a powerful force among believers."[17]

Bishop Margret Wanjiru in a sermon titled "The Roles of the Holy Spirit in our Lives," rejects the personhood of the Holy Spirit and asserts the Holy Spirit as a powerful influence. She states that, "The Holy spirit is the power that dwells inside us to quicken our bodies."[18]

It is worth noting that it is not just neo-Pentecostals alone who hold to the notion of the Holy Spirit as impersonal spirit, but other denominations too have a similar misconception. For example the Seventh-day Adventists (SDA) church has always understood the Holy Spirit as an impersonal divine manifestation of God the Father and of the Son, which on its own does not have a distinct personality. In 1877, J. H. Waggoner had written of the Holy Spirit as an it rather than a he. He described the Spirit of God as "that awful and mysterious power which proceeds from the throne of the universe."[19] Another SDA by the name Uriah wrote, "In a word it [the Holy Spirit] may, perhaps, best be described as a mysterious influence emanating from the Father and the Son, their representative and the medium of their power."[20] Burt reports that "In 1878, D. M. Canright, in a more argumentative and apologetic two-part article, explicitly rejected the personhood of the Holy Spirit, 'The Holy Spirit is not a person, not an individual, but is an influence or power proceeding from the Godhead.'"[21]

This should suffice to demonstrate the misconception some churches have had on the person of the Holy Spirit.

Mission of the Church in a Postmodern Epoch

Our concern in this section is to demonstrate how postmodern skepticism could cast doubt on the work of the Holy Spirit, leading to misconception of the entire doctrine and eventual idolatry. It will also demonstrate how misconception could lead to further divisions in the church as it did during the medieval period (1054 schism).

---

16. Nyabwari and Kagema, "Charismatic Pentecostal Churches," 28.
17. Nyabwari and Kagema, 28.
18. Wanjiru, "Roles of the Holy Spirit."
19. Burt, "Ellen White and the Personhood," and Kagema.
20. Burt.
21. Burt.

Characteristics of Postmodernity

To understand the philosophy of postmodernism, we need an overview of development of ideas before this particular period. Postmodernity was preceded by modernism, which held that knowledge is derived from scientific and rational thinking rather than religious faith, magic or superstition, and during this period people looked to science and logic to explain the world. Natural disasters such as earthquakes were explained by science rather than as an act of God.[22]

Some of the following thinkers seem to have anticipated postmodernism although they lived during the modern era. For example, Karl Jaspers (1883–1973) "saw value in religion but rejected the exclusivism of traditional Christianity."[23] He "stressed that what often passes for 'objective truth' reflects only the conventional beliefs of the day."[24] He posed the question, "How can one know what is genuine?"[25]

Thiselton notes that Martin Heidegger, stressing the relativism of truth, claims

> . . . that even the seemingly "general" questions of philosophy can be asked only concretely, from the standpoint of where the thinker already is. He or she can philosophize only from within their own pre-existing horizons. A thinker can never completely escape the boundaries and problems imposed by this radical finitude.[26]

Thiselton further notes that,

> Sartre and Camus followed Nietzche in attacking every notion of universal or objective truth as illusory. Whereas Nietzsche saw religion and philosophy as the worst culprits in distinguishing self-interest or group-interest as truth for all, Sartre and Camus also attacked the entrapping constraints of what seemed to pass for truth in the mere conventions of society. The individual must not be deceived into imagining that society's notion of "God," "truth," or "the right thing" holds any necessary validity or constraint for free-thinking individuals.[27]

---

22. Thiselton, "From Existentialism to Post-Modernism," 398.
23. Thiselton, 397.
24. Thiselton, 397.
25. Thiselton, 397.
26. Thiselton, 397.
27. Thiselton, 397–98.

As already stated, these philosophers anticipated the birth of postmodern philosophies. The postmodern era is thought to have begun shortly after World War II. Thiselton states that "But by the late 1950s, a reaction had set in against the confusion between subjectivity (the human person is an agent, not an object) and subjectivism (everything is relative to the wishes and views of the individual)."[28]

Whereas modernity was associated with universal, rational truth claims, especially those put forward by mathematics and science,

> Postmodernism expresses a loss of confidence in any universal truth. All claims to truth are viewed as constructs which only serve the interests of particular groups . . . Society as a whole cannot reach outside the values and supposed truths which it has constructed. Every power-group defines what is "normal" for society in ways which promote its own interests.[29]

Thiselton notes that these philosophical perspectives have "led at the end of the twentieth century into a fragmentation of 'what counts as true' . . . Rational argument becomes reduced to manipulative rhetoric."[30] He goes on to state that "If claims to truth are thought to represent only the manipulative power-play of interest-groups, this generates (understandably) suspicion, conflict and violence. Everything that goes wrong is blamed onto the power-interests of some group."[31]

Both rationalism and empiricism "are responses to the skeptical challenge to knowledge. The skeptic queries the reliability of knowledge, and argues that it is always possible to doubt. Rationalism and empiricism are attempts to cure doubt."[32]

Drawing from Karl Jasper, Martin Heidegger, Sartre, Camus and Nietzsche's positions on the question of truth or universal morality, we can infer that during the modern period, people had referred to religion for morality but during postmodernity, people have turned to science and logic. During the postmodern period, faith is regarded as subjective and thus it has given way to science and logic.

According to Jim Leffel, postmodernism holds that

---

28. Thiselton, 398.
29. Thiselton, 398.
30. Thiselton, 398.
31. Thiselton, 398.
32. E. D. Cook, "Epistemology" in Ferguson, Wright, and Packer, *New Dictionary of Theology*, 225.

reality is in the mind of the beholder. People are not able to think independently because they are defined, "scripted," molded by their culture. We cannot judge things in another culture or another person's life, because our reality may be different from theirs. There is no possibility of "transcultural objectivity." Nothing is ever proven, either by science, history, or any other discipline.[33]

We have thus seen that "postmodern religion considers that there are no universal religious truths or laws, rather, reality is shaped by social, historical and cultural contexts according to the individual, place and or time."[34]

Following this thought of relativism, it may be difficult for a postmodernist to believe in religious truth claims, especially when such claims are disputed by members of the same faith. This makes it difficult to evangelize in such a context.

Justification for Correcting Misconceptions of Pneumatology

Thanks to scientific innovations and technological advancement, the world has become a "global village" and therefore ideologies initially confined to cultural and geographical boundaries (e.g. Europe) have become worldwide phenomena. Thus, in contemporary African societies we have people who have been influenced by postmodern philosophies and are incredulous to religious truth claims or absolutism; they question the validity of religious truth claims.

On the contrary, we have Christian conservatives who believe in religious truth claims as absolutes. We could say these Christian conservatives subscribe to the modern era's philosophy, while skeptics subscribe to postmodernism. These two groups are found both in the mainline churches and in the neo-Pentecostal churches. Their misconception of the person and the work of the Holy Spirit is dangerous to the Christian faith, as noted by Daniel Migliore that "neglect and suspicion of the work of the Holy Spirit has damaging effects on both the Christian life and Christian theology."[35] He observes that this could lead to "distortions in the understanding of God, the doctrine of Scripture, the significance of the natural order, the value of human culture, the interpretation of Christ and his work, the nature of the Church, the freedom of the Christian, and the hope for the final fulfillment of life."[36] Migliore further notes the

---

33. Zadava, "What Is Postodernism," *Learn Religions*.
34. Zadava, "What Is Postodernism," *Learn Religions*.
35. Migliore, *Faith Seeking Understanding*, 166.
36. Migliore, 166.

danger of misconception and neglect of the doctrine of the Holy Spirit in relation to other doctrines. He says,

> When the work of the Holy Spirit is forgotten or suppressed, the power of God is apt to be understood as distant, hierarchical, and coercive; Christocentric faith deteriorates into Christomonism; the authority of Scripture becomes heteronomous; the Church is seen as a rigid power structure in which some members rule over others; and the sacraments degenerate into almost magical rites under the control of a clerical elite.[37]

Misconception of the person of the Holy Spirit easily leads some to tritheism as one could easily regard the three persons of the Godhead as different and worship each one of them as separate gods. Or it could lead into some form of modalistic monarchianism – the idea of only one God revealing himself in various modes. Therefore, understanding who the Holy Spirit is helps in understanding that the work of the Holy Spirit is the work of the very one God.

To understand the person of the Holy Spirit (i.e. his personhood and divinity) we shall locate him in the Trinity, since all divine mysteries have their roots in the Trinity.

Construction of a Trinitarian Pneumatology
The Divinity of the Holy Spirit Based on His Relationship in the Godhead

The divinity of the Holy Spirit can best be understood from the Trinitarian point of view. Understanding the relationship in the Holy Trinity is the sure way of understanding the divinity of the Holy Spirit. Migliore's emphasis on this point states that "To speak of the Holy Spirit in Christian theology is to speak not just of any spirit but of the Spirit of the triune God."[38] He relates the Holy Spirit to the Holy Trinity and states that,

> according to the Trinitarian Christian faith, God is the living God whose eternal being is a dynamic communion of love . . . The three persons of the Trinity are not separate selves living in isolation from each other. Rather, they are so intimately united that they "indwell" each other in a society of love.[39]

---

37. Migliore, 166.
38. Migliore, 169.
39. Migliore, 169.

This concept from the classical view was known as a Trinitarian *perichoresis* (Greek) or *circuminscession* (Latin).[40]

However, it should be clarified that although the three persons of the Trinity are distinct from each other, they are not different in essence. Due to the fact that they indwell one another in the principle of love, it is said, the Father is God, the Son is God and the Holy Spirit is God. John Macquarrie states, "The Spirit is not God without the Logos, nor the Logos without the Spirit, nor both without the Father."[41] The fact that the Father is God and the Son is God and the Holy Spirit is God clearly demonstrates the divinity of the Holy Spirit. Thus, the persons of the Trinity are said to share in essence or substance. For this reason, they too share in the eternity.

Think of God as a family who conceives a child. From eternity, God conceives or generates an idea (Logos) and gives birth (begetting) to it. The Greeks called the Logos the Son of God. This is the concept St. John borrows and uses in his gospel.

The idea of begetting here is not in the manner of human begetting where the parent gives birth but both the activity of conceiving and begetting is *missio ad intra*; the Son remains within the Father. Since the Son is in the Father and the Father is in the Son, the Father breathes the Spirit to the Son by way of spiration and the Son reciprocates in love by breathing back the Spirit to the Father by way of spiration, this is what the council fathers at Toledo meant by the double procession. Whatever proceeds from the other is of the same essence as that which it proceeds from. Therefore, since the Spirit proceeds from both the Father and the Son, it means that the Spirit is of the same essence as the Father and the Son and therefore, the Spirit is God. John Macquarrie sums this up when, in relation to the procession of the Holy Spirit from God the Father, he states "the Spirit is God coming forth into the creation to indwell it and to build it up."[42]

Personhood of the Holy Spirit

Our argument for the personhood of the Holy Spirit aims at correcting the notion that the Spirit is an impersonal divine force (an "it") proceeding from the Godhead. It will also help in demonstrating that the person of the Holy Spirit should not be mistaken for an impersonal force that can be manipulated

---

40. Nyamiti, *Jesus Christ, the Ancestor*, 79.
41. Macquarrie, *Principles of Christian Theology*, 329.
42. Macquarrie, 328.

or commanded but is to be revered on the same level as God the Father and God the Son.

We shall use biblical Greek grammar and biblical accounts to argue for the personhood of the Holy Spirit. The personhood of the Holy Spirit has been contested by certain groups of people in the history of the church, arguing that since the noun for "spirit" (*pneuma*) as used especially in the New Testament is neuter, therefore, the Spirit should be referred to as an "it" rather than he or she.[43] This led to such groups drifting to gnostic tendencies of referring to the Holy Spirit as an active force of God.[44] However, this idea has been contested on the grounds that there is no "connection in Koine Greek between grammatical gender and personal gender so it is simply false to say that since the Greek noun *pneuma* is neuter the spirit must be an 'it.'"[45]

In John 14:16 Jesus promises his disciples that he would send them another just like himself. The Greek rendering is *allos*, which means one just like himself. From this it is possible to conclude that the *allos* was a person since Jesus himself was a person.[46] Jesus further referred to this *allos* as *parakletos*. *Parakletos* from Greek rendition means an enabler, comforter and encourager.[47] Since such functions can only be performed by a person, it is logical to conclude that indeed the *parakletos* was a person just like Jesus that had come to continue his ministry and not an "it" or a mere force.

Greg Herrick, summarizes scriptural texts that allude to the personhood of the Holy Spirit and avers that:

> ... the fact that the Spirit makes choices (1 Cor 12:11), teaches (John 14:26), guides (John 16:13), reveals Jesus (John 16:14), convicts (John 16:8), seals believers (2 Cor 1:21–22), can be grieved (Eph 4:30), blasphemed (Matt 12:31), possesses a rational mind (Rom 8:26–27; 1 Cor 2:11–13), can be lied to (Acts 5:3–4), quenched (1 Thess 5:19), resisted (Acts 7:51) and on numerous occasions is distinguished from, yet directly linked with, the Father and the Son as co-worker and co-recipient of worship, argues definitively for his personhood (Matt 28:19–20; 2 Cor 13:14).[48]

---

43. Herrick, "Pneumatology," Bible.org.
44. According to the gnostics, the Spirit was an active force emanating from one, true God.
45. Herrick, "Pneumatology."
46. Herrick.
47. Herrick.
48. Herrick.

From the foregoing arguments, we conclude that the Spirit of God is God in the same manner God the Father is God and God the Son is God and is also a person. How then can the person and the work of the Holy Spirit be communicated in the context of postmodern skepticism? Ontological-existentialism shall form our conceptual framework.

Ontological-Existential

Functional theologians would begin their theologizing from anthropological points. For example Karl Rahner, Bernerd Lonegarn and John Macquarrie all begin from the human experience. Their argument is that theology begins with human experience toward reflection on God. According to Karl Rahner, the starting point for theology (God-human relationship) is "nothing less than human experience taken as a whole."[49] He argues that as human beings, we have experience:

> we experience ourselves as people in time and place. . . . we can only ask questions limited to this horizon . . . our perspective of knowledge is limited by this horizon . . . yet for all our limitations, human persons seem to go beyond time and place to grasp the meaning of life itself. . . . Through knowledge acquired through asking questions, the human person goes beyond himself or herself to the meaning of life itself as grasped within my particular history.[50]

According, to Bernard Lonergan, "If definition of theology is faith seeking understanding, then we must pay attention to how we know, what we know, when we know, and how we know that we know. Human knowing is the place to begin."[51] He goes further to state that "The dynamic process of knowing always operates the same way: experience, understanding, judging, and deciding."[52]

Macquarrie's approach is the existential-ontological method.[53] In this approach, "the present moment is the starting point of their analysis."[54] The functional theologians (Lonergan, Macquarrie and Rahner) begin by analyzing

---

49. Mueller, *What Are They Saying*, 7.
50. Mueller, 7.
51. Mueller, 7.
52. Mueller, 7.
53. Mueller, 22.
54. Mueller, 22.

"the changing existential situation for which all manners and means of contemporary scientific knowledge can be used."[55] In his existential-ontological approach he uses the parable of the prodigal son to deconstruct the classical objective views of atonement and introduces the subjective view. He argues that it was not until the prodigal son became aware of a disorder in his own existence that he remembered the love of the father and turned away from his sinful life and resolved to return to the father. Back home the father is depicted as waiting for the return of the son.[56]

His position of beginning from the human point of view is premised on understanding that human beings' existence is unique; it is not like that of other creatures. This is because their existence has been disclosed to them. They know that they are.[57] Based on this understanding, he explains that the prodigal son realized his state of existence and turned. However, in Reformed theology, God is the first mover in the process of salvation. It is God who enables humans to repent and turn back to him. Therefore, it is only logical to argue that God acts and human beings react. Human reaction here is understood as a faithful ascend to God's revelation. God acts, humans react because God's action is never contingent to human action. This process is what we shall call ontological-existential. The human ability to respond to God's appeal is because God has enabled it.

A Critique of Either a Purely Ontological or a Purely Functional Pneumatology

Glendon Thompson notes that Jean-Luc Marion, a postmodern deconstructive theologian, criticizes ontotheology (the theology of being) on grounds that "language of being limits the divine."[58] He goes further to describe the classical theism of an infinite, invisible and immutable God as a form of conceptual idol. He would advocate for a conception of God as love and as superabundant gift. He "qualifies, however, that although God gifts himself freely, human beings cannot dominate the gift."[59] In other words, thinking of God in very abstract terms removes him from the reality of his interaction in human history. Yet even with God's condescendence, human beings cannot dominate his gift and

---

55. Mueller, 23.
56. Macquarrie, *Principles of Christian Theology*, 311–27.
57. Macquarrie, 60.
58. Thompson, "Postmodern Theology." https://www.thegospelcoalition.org/essay/postmodern-theology/.
59. Thompson.

they cannot monopolize or cage such gifts. This position is supported by John Caputo who employs the term "impossible" for God and concludes that while individuals may experience the divine, they cannot know him – "We do not know what we believe or to whom we are praying."[60]

The less radical theologians aver that God should not be removed from the reality of human life. They consider

> triune relationships as a social trinity (a non-hierarchical, co-equal, and reciprocal community). These thinkers also downplay divine transcendence, while emphasizing divine immanence. For them, the weak and vulnerable God exists in a dynamic, mutually dependent, and pantheistic relationship with creation.[61]

Regarding pure functional pneumatology, we can say, just as much as ontological pneumatology impoverishes the ability of the divine mystery, by limiting it to the being, functional pneumatology would limit the divine to anthropology and thus impoverish its ability to transcend time and space. A functional pneumatology limits the divine to specific places (churches) and to specific functions (e.g. speaking in tongues).

Theological Reflection on Trinitarian Pneumatology as a Panacea

In an attempt to use Trinitarian pneumatology as a solution to resolving the conflict of doubt caused by postmodern skeptics, whether speaking in tongues could be evidence of being indwelt by the Holy Spirit, we have to note that skepticism deals with "the relationship between objectivity and subjectivity, in terms of whether we can know something totally objectively and to what extent subjectivity intrudes or is seen to be problematic."[62] We should also note that "Christianity is not simply a question of faith, but also one of knowledge."[63] Therefore, would we say the experience of the Holy Spirit is subjective or objective? Would the failure to demonstrate empirically one's experience of the work of the Holy Spirit in their life render that experience inauthentic? How does the ontological foundation of pneumatology resolve the postmodern skepticism on the person and the work of the Holy Spirit in the life of a believer?

---

60. Thompson.
61. Thompson.
62. E. D. Cook, "Epistemology" in Ferguson, Wright, and Packer, *New Dictionary of Theology*, 225.
63. Cook, "Epistemology," 225.

We shall locate our discussions in the idea of revelation and human response as a faithful ascend to God's revelation.

Infilling by the Holy Spirit and Response

We should note that revelation is of two natures: general and special. General (or natural) revelation "looks to the nature of the world and the nature of humanity as revealing something of the nature of God. [God] may be known by deducing his nature from the world or humanity."[64] Special revelation is where God reveals himself in a "special" way to particular people, for example in the call of prophets and through divine mysteries like incarnation, resurrection and miracles. Through these events God reveals something about his nature.[65] God revealed himself to the prophets by way of pouring out his Spirit into them. This infilling by the Holy Spirit is the process by which God reveals himself to his creation. Infilling by the Holy Spirit is what we shall regard as the self-donation of God or revelation.

Mueller observes that "Theologically Rahner characterizes a human being as a hearer of the word."[66] He elaborates that "hearing goes beyond sound to the personal encounter of a presence. What we hear are not words but God's own self communicated."[67] Using an analogy of two people who fall in love, Rahner states, "oneself hears or encounters another self in free self-donation . . . God donates (communicates) grace. The result is mutual self-donation which is love."[68] In the reciprocal self-donation, the human being responds with love. Thus, the mutual self-donation here is that of grace and love.

This reciprocation is possible because in the God-human relation, human beings are open to God. "We are open to the mystery which grounds all meaning. This mystery is God."[69] Rahner goes on to explain that, "The human person [is] radically (i.e., 'from the roots') open to God . . . they have the capacity to go beyond themselves ('trans')."[70] The going beyond the self is possible through knowledge and freedom. Through this openness, the human person becomes "the arena where the encounter with God takes place

---

64. Cook, "Epistemology," 225–26.

65. Cook, 225–26.

66. Rahner, *Hearer of the Word* (New York: Herder and Herder, 1972) quoted in Mueller, *What Are They Saying*, 9.

67. Mueller, 9–10.

68. Mueller, 10.

69. Mueller, 7.

70. Mueller, 7.

(theological anthropology)."[71] Therefore, "If our humanity is the medium through which God communicates with us, then what is said about us says something about God who is involved with us."[72]

The ontological-existential process here is that the first step is God's self-donation, the second step is a human encounter of the grace of God, the third is human reflection on the encounter and then last is human response. Human response to God's revelation (understanding) may differ from one person to another and may also lead to any of the gifts stated in scripture (cf. 1 Cor 12:1–11) or to a numinous awe that leads to silence. This is transcendental from an ontological point in that God pours down the God-self (grace) into the human heart, the human heart is warmed up and rises (transcends) to reflect on that experience (encounter), which brings the human being to understanding the revelation (God's self-donation). Therefore, we are saying that the Holy Spirit is God, and when God enters us we are inspired to yield the various gifts as listed by Paul, and therefore it is illogical to dismiss anyone who claims they are indwelt by the Holy Spirit when the said gifts are evident. Nonetheless, gifts such as gifts of faith, healing, wisdom and discernment cannot be verbalized even when they are present in one who is indwelt.[73]

Difficulty of Explaining the Experience
We have already alluded to the fact that religious knowledge is of a radically different sort from that which we find in other fields of human experience like science. If rationalists and empiricists demand that truth claims should be logical and empirical respectively, then religious claims could easily be falsified. However, Macquarrie argues that, since theological language is non-logical, non-verifiable and inexpressible, because it is mythological, analogical and symbolical and all these cannot be verifiable,[74] it is not realistic to subject its truth claims to empirical or rational verifications.

For example, how would one verify one's claim that they are born again, or saved, or that their speaking in tongues is evidence of being indwelt by the Holy Spirit? What does that mean to a person of another faith? Such claims may mean nothing to a person of another faith who may demand empirical verification or logical demonstration. But does failure to demonstrate the claim empirically or logically make the experience false? These claims undoubtedly

---

71. Mueller, 6.
72. Mueller, 6.
73. See also Jorstad, *Holy Spirit in Today's Church*, 77–134.
74. Macquarrie, *Principles of Christian Theology*, 129.

mean something to the one who makes them, and no one else can understand what is meant unless they share in the faith or experience. Therefore, in order to understand or discern the indwelling of the Holy Spirit one has to participate in the faith. The answer lies in faith and not in empiricism or rationalism.

This brings us to the conclusion that faith, and faith as a commitment, must precede our talking about religious experience, and we realize that what we say cannot be proved but that does not mean that the experience has not taken place. Religious statements express a way of understanding the world. They include an element of faith and of commitment on the part of the Christians, which cannot be usually verified until the hereafter.[75] Macquarrie says, "The meaning of a language has to be looked for in the way it gets used."[76] He goes further to state that,

> The justification of theological language is to be sought precisely by putting it in the context of the experiences which give rise to it. These are the experiences of the community of faith, in which men [and women] move from the questioning of their own being to the search for meaning and to the revelatory experience in which they are grasped by the grace of being.[77]

The answer to this difficulty lies in our ontological-existential approach. In this top-down approach Jesus

> as the image of the invisible God (Col 1:15), he is the revealer of God's love par excellence; as human, he is the hearer of God's word par excellence. Thus if we want to know what God is like and how he has involved himself with us, then we look to Jesus. Likewise if we want to know what humanity is like and how we are involved in God, then we look to Jesus. Using spatial imagery, whether our perspective is from the divine above or from the human below, Jesus Christ is the unique meeting place of the God-human relationship.[78]

---

75. R. L. Sturch, "Religious Language," in *New Dictionary of Theology* (England: Inter-Varsity Press, 1988), 579.
76. Macquarrie, *Principles of Christian Theology*, 124.
77. Macquarrie, 125.
78. Mueller, *What Are They Saying*, 8.

Pastoral and Transformative Implications of Ontological-Existential Approach

So far, we have noted that misconception of pneumatology leads to heresies, idolatry and schism in the church. With clarification of this doctrine using the doctrine of Trinity, idolatry will be minimized, churches will not conflict on the question of the Holy Spirit indwelling some people and not others, since they will have understood that the Holy Spirit is God and God is in all churches that call upon him, and anxiety is assuaged among those who thought because they did not speak in tongues the Holy Spirit did not indwell them.

Conclusion

This paper has demonstrated that misconception of the person and work of the Holy Spirit could lead to heresies, idolatry and schism. We have also noted that postmodern skepticism has permeated society and the church, they demand logical or empirical evidence to every truth claim. The paper also demonstrated that religious knowledge and language do not belong to our normal knowledge and language. We also noted that the Holy Spirit is God and that the work of the Holy Spirit on earth is the mission of God on earth (*missio Dei* or *missio ad extra*).

Based on the fact that the Holy Spirit is God and God is Spirit (cf. John 4:24), we have argued that when we speak of being indwelt by the Holy Spirit, it means we are speaking of being indwelt by God. Since God is Spirit we cannot demand empirical evidence of being indwelt. Therefore, manifestation of any of the gifts listed in 1 Corinthians 12:1–11 is sufficient evidence of being indwelt.

Bibliography

Anderson, Allan, Michael Bergunder, André Droogers, and Cornelis van der Laan, eds. *Studying Global Pentecostalism: Theories and Methods*. Berkeley: University of California Press, 2010.

Anglican Church of Kenya. *Our Modern Services*. Nairobi: Uzima Press, 2003.

Burt, Merlin D. "Ellen White and the Personhood of the Holy Spirit." *Ministry* (April 2012). Available online, https://www.ministrymagazine.org/archive/2012/04/ellen-white-and-the-personhood-of-the-holy-spirit.

Cook, E. D. "Epistemology" in Ferguson, Wright, and Packer, *New Dictionary of Theology*. Downers Grove: InterVarsity Press, 1988.

Davids, J. Steven. "The Importance of Athanasius and the Views of His Character." PhD diss., Liberty University, 2017. Available online, https://digitalcommons.liberty.edu/cgi/viewcontent.cgi?article=2678&context=doctoral.

Ferguson, Sinclair B., David F. Wright, and J. I. Packer, eds. *New Dictionary of Theology*. Downers Grove: InterVarsity Press, 1988.

Herrick, Greg. "Pneumatology: The Holy Spirit." *Bible.org*, An Introduction to Christian Belief: A Layman's Guide series. https://bible.org/seriespage/4-pneumatology-holy-spirit. https://bible.org/seriespage/4-pneumatology-holy-spirit.

Hillyer, P. N. "Religious Experience," in *New Dictionary of Theology*, edited by Sinclair B. Ferguson, David F. Wright, and J. I. Packer, 577–79. Downers Grove: InterVarsity Press, 1988.

Jorstad, Erling, ed. *The Holy Spirit in Today's Church: A Handbook of the New Pentecostalism*. Nashville: Abingdon, 1973.

Keith, G. A. "Arianism" in Ferguson, Wright, and Packer, *New Dictionary of Theology*.

Macquarrie, John. *Principles of Christian Theology*. London: SCM Press, 1977.

Migliore, L. Daniel. *Faith Seeking Understanding: An Introduction to Christian Theology*. Grand Rapids: Eerdmans, 1991.

Mueller, J. J. *What Are They Saying About Theological Method?* New York: Paulist Press, 1984.

Nyabwari, Bernard Gechiko, and Dickson Nkonge Kagema. "Charismatic Pentecostal Churches in Kenya: Growth, Culture and Orality." *International Journal of Humanities Social Sciences and Education* 1, no. 3 (March 2014): 27–33.

Nyamiti, Charles. *Jesus Christ, the Ancestor of Humankind: Methodological and Trinitarian Foundations*. Nairobi: CUEA Publications, 2005.

Parsitau, Damaris Seleina. "The Civic and Public Roles of Neo-Pentecostal Churches in Kenya (1970–2010)" (Unpublished Doctoral Thesis submitted at Kenyatta University, 2014), 1–454.

Parsitau, Damaris Seleina, and Philomena Njeri Mwaura, "God in the City: Pentecostalism as an urban Phenomenon in Kenya," *Sudia Historiae Ecclesiasticae*, October 2010, 36 (2): 95–112.

Rahner, Karl. *Hearer of the Word: Laying the Foundation for a Philosophy of Religion*. New York: Herder and Herder, 1972.

Sturch, R. L. "Religious language" in *New Dictionary of Theology*, edited by Sinclair B. Ferguson, David F. Wright, and J. I. Packer, 579–80. Downers Grove: InterVarsity Press, 1988.

Thiselton, C. Anthony. "From Existentialism to Post-Modernism." In *Eerdmans' Handbook to the World's Religions*, edited by R. P. Beaver, 396–98. Grand Rapids: Eerdmans, 1994.

Thompson, Glednond. "Postmodern Theology." *The Gospel Coalition*, Concise Theology series. https://www.thegospelcoalition.org/essay/postmodern-theology/.

Wanjiru, Margaret. "Bishop Margaret Wanjiru – The Roles of the Holy Spirit in Our Lives." Sermon posted on 27 February 2014. YouTube video, https://youtu.be/kzigavy0c98?t=514.

"What Was the Pneumatomachian Heresy / Macedonianism?" *Got Questions*, last updated 4 January 2022. https://www.gotquestions.org/Pneumatomachian-Macedonianism.html.

Wright, David F. "Councils and Creeds" in *A Lion Handbook: The History of Christianity*, Oxford: Lion Publishing, 1977, 172.

Zadava, Jack. "What Is Postmodernism in Religion?" *Learn Religions*, Abrahamic/Middle Eastern, Christianity. Last updated 2 February 2019. https://www.learnreligions.com/what-is-postmodernism-700692.

5

In Dialogue with the Jehovah's Witnesses

The "Name" of the Holy Spirit

Jeffrey S. Krohn

Professor of Biblical Studies, Evangelical Theological College, Addis Ababa, Ethiopia

Abstract

The Jehovah's Witnesses contend that the Holy Spirit has no name. Since the possession of a name is considered to be an essential characteristic of a person, they further contend that the Spirit is some*thing* and not some*one*. Many thinkers counter this assertion. They argue that "the Holy Spirit" is, in fact, his name. They also affirm the possible names of "the Spirit" or "the Paraclete." Nonetheless, I do not think that these are adequate responses to the contention of the Jehovah's Witnesses. This chapter explores *the possibility* that the Spirit has no name (in Scripture). I will propose three possible responses to defend this biblical lacuna. One response focuses on the exaltation of Christ by the Spirit. The Spirit directs attention toward Christ – and away from himself. If a name for the Spirit was included in Scripture, this might distract from this important christological focus. A second response notes the biblical "equivalency" between the Spirit and Christ. A name for the Holy Spirit, if given, might have blurred the laser focus of this "equivalency." (While Christ and the Spirit are not the same person, there is some type of equivalency between them.) A third response highlights the title of "the Holy Spirit." While at times the Scriptures simply call him the Spirit, there seems to be an emphasis on referring to him as the *Holy* Spirit. This is a potential reason for his apparent lack of name – to focus on his primary ministry, that of sanctification or making us holy. Instead of exhibiting his identity through the mention of his name, then, Scripture illustrates his identity through his focus on (and exaltation of) Christ, his equivalency with Christ and his work of sanctification.

Key words: name of the Holy Spirit, Jehovah's Witnesses, personhood of the Holy Spirit, exaltation of Christ, sanctification

The "Name" of the Holy Spirit

There exists a variety of perspectives on the "name" of the Holy Spirit. The Jehovah's Witnesses believe that the Holy Spirit does not have a name and consequently is not a person. They refer to the Spirit as an "it" (something) and not with "he" (someone). The denial of the Trinity – three persons in one God – follows from this argument. Others maintain that he does, in fact, have a name – "the Holy Spirit." Since I sympathize with the Jehovah's Witnesses concerning the issue of a name, I would like to explore the possibility that, in fact, the Holy Spirit does *not* have a name, at least one mentioned in Scripture (I unequivocally disagree with them, however, on their denial of his personhood, as well as their denial of the Trinity). Again, I emphasize merely the exploration of *the possibility* that he does not have a name in Scripture. There would be, I believe, valid reasons for this scriptural absence. This discussion has particular relevance given that a "dominant theological theme in contemporary African Christianity is pneumatology."[1] Furthermore, an important emphasis of the evangelical doctrine concerning the Holy Spirit is his personhood. For this chapter, space will not allow for a comprehensive defense of his personhood. Nonetheless, his personhood will be a logical implication of the following discussion points. The overall goal of this chapter is to explore plausible arguments for the lack of a name of the Holy Spirit in the biblical record, while maintaining that he is the "third *person*" of the Triune God. The argument will center on three biblical emphases: the exaltation of Christ by the Spirit; the equivalency between Christ and the Spirit; and the focus on the Spirit's primary "ministry" of sanctification. First, however, it is necessary to highlight several introductory matters.

---

1. Tonghou Ngong, "Who Is the Holy Spirit," 313.

Doctrine of the Jehovah's Witnesses

The Jehovah's Witnesses claim nearly nine million members worldwide.[2] In East Africa, there are over 11,000 Kingdom Halls.[3] The Witnesses allege that the Holy Spirit "is not a person but is a powerful force that God causes to emanate from himself to accomplish his holy will (Ps 104:30; 2 Pet 1:21; Acts 4:31)."[4] A widely-used booklet by the Witnesses argues that in "the Bible, the use of the expression 'holy spirit' indicates that it is a controlled force that Jehovah God uses to carry out various purposes."[5] This "invisible active force" is sent forth "to accomplish what is holy. So it is correctly called 'holy spirit.'"[6] Furthermore, the Witnesses assert, "The Bible gives the names of Jehovah God and of his Son, Jesus Christ; yet, nowhere does it name the holy spirit (Isaiah 42:8; Luke 1:31)."[7]

Further declarations by the Witnesses cast doubt on the personhood of the Spirit. For example, they describe different "things" in Scripture that are personified: sin, wisdom and death (Gen 4:7; Luke 7:35; Rom 5:14, 21). Similarly, there is the personification of water and blood that "testify" (1 John 5:7-8). The conclusion, for the Witnesses, is that the holy spirit, as a "thing," is also personified. Additionally, the holy spirit is grouped (or "paralleled") with impersonal "things" like wisdom (Acts 6:3), faith (Acts 11:24), joy (Acts 13:52), love (2 Cor 6:6) and deep conviction (1 Thess 1:5).[8] The implication is that the spirit is also a "thing." These arguments deny the personhood of the Holy Spirit. My main response, however, will center on the issue of a name for the Holy Spirit. Nevertheless, these assertions of the Witnesses will be indirectly addressed in my discussion.

---

2. Watchtower Bible and Tract Society, "Jehovah's Witnesses Around the World."
3. Watchtower Bible and Tract Society, "Jehovah's Witnesses Around the World." Zambia, with 3,528 congregations, has the highest concentration. Other countries include South Sudan with 33 congregations, Ethiopia with 215, Kenya with 651, Malawi with 1,718, and Rwanda with 571.
4. Watchtower Bible and Tract Society, *Reasoning from the Scriptures*, 381; cf. 406–7.
5. Watchtower Bible and Tract Society, *Should You Believe in the Trinity?*, 20.
6. Watchtower Bible and Tract Society, *Holy Spirit – The Force Behind the Coming New Order!*, 11.
7. Watchtower Bible and Tract Society, "What Is the Holy Spirit?"
8. Watchtower, *Reasoning from the Scriptures*, 21–22.

The "Opaqueness" Surrounding the Spirit

In some ways, the argumentation concerning the Spirit is understandable. For Ferguson, the mention of the

> Holy Spirit . . . tends to convey a cold, even remote image. After all, what is "Spirit"? Yet, perhaps the older "Holy Ghost," with its connotations of vagueness, mystery and insubstantiality, did in fact express what many Christians experience: the Holy Spirit is seen to be distant and impersonal by comparison with the Father and the Son.[9]

In addition, the enigmatic work of the Spirit is compared with the wind in the Gospel of John: "The wind blows wherever it pleases. You hear its sound, but you cannot tell where it comes from or where it is going. So it is with everyone born of the Spirit" (John 3:8). The Spirit's work can be characterized as "mysterious."[10] The challenging phrase of the "seven spirits of God" (Rev 1:4; 3:1; 4:5; 5:6) adds to this opaqueness. Finally, as the Witnesses pointed out, it is noteworthy that Scripture specifically describes the contexts where the Father is named (Exod 3:13–15; Isa 42:8) and where the Son is named (Matt 1:21, 25). There is no corresponding passage where the Spirit is "named" – at least with the specific words for "name" in Hebrew (*shem*) or Greek (*onoma*), such as in the verses for the Father and the Son.

We mentioned above a few reasons why the Witnesses believe the Spirit is not a person. Other "impersonal" descriptions in Scripture include the following. There are various "representations of the Holy Spirit," like clothing (Luke 24:49), a dove (Luke 3:22), a pledge/ deposit (2 Cor 1:22; Eph 1:14), fire (Acts 2:3), a seal (2 Cor 1:22; Eph 1:13; 4:30) and water (John 7:37–39).[11] In Genesis 2:7, we note that God "breathed into [Adam's] nostrils the breath of life." This impersonal word "breath" can also be translated as "spirit."[12] Biblically, the word translated Spirit

> is the Greek word *pneuma* (the equivalent of its Hebrew counterpart, *rûaḥ*) whose fundamental meaning is "air in motion." This word encompasses such ideas as wind, gale, storm or blast

---

9. Ferguson, *Holy Spirit*, 15.
10. Ferguson, 123.
11. Enns, *Moody Handbook of Theology*, 253–56.
12. Assohoto, "Genesis," 13.

(see Exod 14:21; 15:8; Gen 1:2) . . . [and] may also be used to describe something as gentle as a breeze (see Gen 3:8).[13]

At the very least, then, given the impersonal nature of *rûaḥ* and *pneuma* as wind or air, there seems to be a difference in the titles and names of the three persons of the Trinity – especially as we recognize the *personal* nature of the names of "Father" and "Son." Again, I affirm the personhood of the Holy Spirit – however, this biblical evidence of impersonal traits adds to the opaqueness concerning the Spirit.

As a response to the potential obscurity and opaqueness of this issue, I will briefly suggest two trajectories for possible future study, both of which are potential answers to the perspective of Jehovah's Witnesses. These trajectories assert a name for the Holy Spirit. I do not believe, however, that these trajectories are an adequate response to their arguments. Nonetheless, these trajectories constitute a foundation-building exercise as we consider the complexity surrounding this issue. Following these trajectories, I will defend my proposal.

The Holy Spirit Has a Name

Some authors affirm the existence of a name for the Holy Spirit. For Basil of Caesarea, "Holy Spirit" is his "chief and distinguishing name."[14] R. A. Torrey writes of "the name of the Holy Spirit" seen in 2 Corinthians 13:14 and Matthew 28:19.[15] He also speaks of "at least twenty-five different names [that] are used in the Old and New Testaments in speaking of the Holy Spirit."[16] Such names (or titles) include, "Paraclete" (John 14:16, 26; 15:26); "the promise of the Father" (Acts 1:4; 2:33); "the Spirit of life" (Rev 11:11 NIV footnote); "the Spirit of truth" (1 John 4:6); "the Spirit of grace" (Heb 10:29); "the eternal Spirit" (Heb 9:14); "the Spirit of glory" (1 Pet 4:14); "the Spirit of prophecy" (Rev 19:10); and even "the anointing" (1 John 2:27, cf. 2:20).[17] Author A. S. Wood writes that "the Spirit" is mentioned forty-six times in the New Testament; "the Spirit of God" eighteen times; and "the Spirit of the Lord" four times. Yet he concludes,

---

13. Hawthorne, "Holy Spirit," 489.
14. See *De Spiritu Sancto*, 9.22; cf. O'Collins, *Tripersonal God*, 190.
15. Torrey, *Person and Work of the Holy Spirit*, 30–31.
16. Torrey, 39.
17. See Hawthorne, "Holy Spirit," 490.

"The title 'Holy Spirit' is by far the most common."[18] John Frame expands the idea and includes the other members of the Trinity with "the threefold name of God . . . Father, Son, and Holy Spirit (2 Cor 13:14)."[19] Ambrose wrote that the "name of the Father, Son and Spirit is one." He emphasized the singular "name" in contradistinction to the possibility of plural "names." He further argued that the Son and the Father have the same name ("the Lord," see Exod 33:19; John 5:43), and that the name of the Son is equated with the name of the Spirit ("another Paraclete," John 14:16; cf. 1 John 2:1).[20] P. K. Jewett agrees, since the Spirit has "a personal name . . . he is the other Comforter or Paraclete (John 14:16–26)."[21] Thus, given these various perspectives, many affirm a name (or names) for the Holy Spirit. Despite these views, however, going forward I will proceed with the assumption that "the Holy Spirit" is a title, and not a name.[22]

Another trajectory that defends a name (or names) for the Holy Spirit centers on the entire biblical witness surrounding the "name" of God. We note, for example, the centrality of Yahweh's name in the Hebrew Scriptures: "This is my name forever, the name by which I am to be remembered from generation to generation" (Exod 3:15; cf. 6:3, 7; 15:3; 23:21; 34:5–7; Lev 24:11; Deut 28:58; Ps 30:4; 83:18; 96:2; 97:12; 135:13; 145:21; Isa 42:8; Jer 16:21; 33:2; Hos 12:5). In addition, Ezekiel tells us that Yahweh acts "for the sake of [his] holy name," and that he "will show the holiness of [his] great name" (Ezek 36:21–23). The importance of the name of Jesus in the New Testament continues this biblical witness, given that believers are washed, sanctified, and justified "*in the name of the Lord Jesus Christ*" (1 Cor 6:11; cf. Matt 1:21, 25; Luke 2:21; 24:47; John 1:12; 17:11–12; 20:31; Acts 4:12; 15:26; 1 Cor 1:10). Furthermore, at the climax of redemptive history, we note the aforementioned singular (not plural) "name"

---

18. Wood, "Holiness," 188. Notice that Wood calls the "Holy Spirit" a title. As we will see below, "Holy Spirit" is mentioned over ninety times.

19. Frame, *Salvation Belongs to the Lord*, 160.

20. Ambrose of Milan, "Three Books of St. Ambrose on the Holy Spirit," 1.13. 127–33 (NPNF 2/10: 110–11).

21. Jewett, "Holy Spirit," 192.

22. See the words of Craig Keener: "Although used only twice in the Old Testament (Ps 51; Is 63), this term [of the Holy Spirit] became a common *title* for the Spirit of God in New Testament times" (Keener, *IVP Bible Background Commentary*, 782, emphasis added). Relatedly, in the "Great Commission," we note "Father, Son, and Holy Spirit" with three definite articles (denoting plurality), all subsumed under "the name" (denoting singularity): τὸ ὄνομα τοῦ πατρὸς καὶ τοῦ υἱοῦ καὶ τοῦ ἁγίου πνεύματος ("the name of the Father and of the Son and of the Holy Spirit"). Could this biblical phrase be evidence more for the defense of the unity within the plurality of the Godhead, rather than an affirmation of a specific name for the Holy Spirit? It is interesting, and important to note, that Matt 28:19 does not say "in the *names* of the Father, Son and Holy Spirit."

of the Father, Son and Holy Spirit (Matt 28:19). Thus, a focus on the entire biblical trajectory of the "name" of God could be a response to this possible lack of a personal name for the Holy Spirit. There would not be a "need" for a specific name of the Holy Spirit, given this thorough biblical trajectory of the "name" of God.

A similar angle by Leupp focuses on God as Trinity: "Every way that God has of being God, the totality of God's self-awareness and expression, is summed up in the Trinity. The Trinity is the fullness of God, the length and breadth and depth of all that God is."[23] Leupp concludes that "from everlasting to everlasting God's name is triune. God does not have three names; God has one name 'above all names,' uttered in three distinct yet inseparable ways, God's thrice-blessed name . . . God's name is triune. God is the Triune God."[24] However, while Leupp maintains this "one name," he also mentions "the classical *names* of God: Father, Son and Holy Spirit."[25] He writes that we should exercise great caution here and continue to emphasize "Father, Son and Holy Spirit," since the phrase is "biblical speech" and has been used throughout the centuries in the Christian church.[26] Nonetheless, he adds that while "new names for God . . . are well documented in Scripture . . . (e.g. Lover, Friend, Abba, Servant and Paraclete) . . . [these] neglected themes will not eliminate the traditional names but, positively, will supplement and illuminate all of Christian life and thought."[27] Author O'Collins agrees that the "primary" way of speaking about God is "Father, Son and Holy Spirit," yet he contends that it is not the "exclusive" way "of speaking about the tripersonal God."[28] At the very least, the complexity of this discussion is illustrated with these competing ideas of a "name" or "names." To summarize, these two trajectories – the title "Holy Spirit" as his name and the biblical witness to the "name" that encompasses the three persons of the Father, Son and Spirit – are possible rejoinders to the arguments of Jehovah's Witnesses. However, there are other potential responses.

---

23. Leupp, *Knowing the Name of God*, 15.
24. Leupp, 13–14.
25. Leupp, 46, emphasis added.
26. Leupp, 46.
27. Leupp, 49. If other names are used, Leupp states that "we must only be certain that however we address God, respect, worship and love are what most motivates us" and that names "must be finally rooted in the Bible" (Leupp, 48).
28. O'Collins, *Tripersonal God*, 185.

The Holy Spirit Has No Name

Although I will not dogmatically proclaim that the Holy Spirit has no (specific) name, I will at least advance plausible biblical reasons for the lack of a name. Relevant and important introductory considerations of "name" include the following. Why is the third person referred to as "Spirit" rather than another Son?[29] Is this use of language alerting us to something important, given the personal nature of the word "Son"? Why are there various "names" for *all three members* of the Trinity? The first person of the Trinity is referred to as Father (Matt 28:19);[30] Yahweh (Exod 3:14–15);[31] "Abba" (Mark 14:36; Rom 8:15; Gal 4:16), or simply "God."[32] The second person of the Trinity is referred to as the Son (Matt 28:19); Jesus (Matt 1:21, 25); the Paraclete (1 John 2:1); the Word (John 1:1, 14); and the firstborn (Rom 8:29; Col 1:15, 18).[33] For the third person of the Trinity, Scripture mentions "the Spirit" more than two hundred times; "Holy Spirit" approximately ninety times;[34] and other titles (mentioned above) such as "Spirit of truth" (1 John 4:6), or "the eternal Spirit" (Heb 9:14). Should his name be "the Spirit," since that appears over twice as many times as "the Holy Spirit"? Is it possible to conclude that all three members have more than "one name"? At the very least, and with a reminder of the "the classical names" of the Father, Son, and Holy Spirit that we saw above, it is noteworthy that each member clearly has multiple names/titles.[35] Finally, if "Holy Spirit" is his name, why is an adjective ("holy") part of his name? Why do we *not* see adjectives in the name of the Father and the Son? In sum, the complexity of the issue is witnessed with these introductory considerations. I will now explore three biblical emphases that might illuminate the discussion: the exaltation of Christ by the Spirit; the equivalency between Christ and the Spirit; and the focus on the Spirit's primary "ministry." These emphases might give us reasons for the lack of a name of the Holy Spirit.

---

29. See Lewis and Demarest, *Integrative Theology*, 278.

30. More than twenty times, "God is named as Father in the OT . . . 'Father' is used 254 times in the NT" (O'Collins, *Tripersonal God*, 14, 185).

31. "YHWH . . . [is used] about 6,800 times in the OT" (O'Collins, *Tripersonal God*, 14).

32. "'God' . . . (*ho theos*) . . . [is] the name with which the NT often designates God the Father" (O'Collins, *Tripersonal God*, 186).

33. In fact, there are "well over 100 distinctive names for Jesus in the NT alone" (O'Collins, *Tripersonal God*, 186).

34. Strong, *Enhanced Strong's Lexicon*, #4151.

35. This assertion appears to contradict my stated argument. My aim, however, is merely to point out the complexity of the situation by detailing the multiple names/titles of all three members of the Trinity.

Exaltation of Christ

The work of the Spirit in the New Testament era and beyond is intimately linked to the exaltation of Christ. This work seems so prominent that it might be possible to connect the Spirit's identity with this exaltation of Christ. The Spirit "selflessly glorifies the Son."[36] As part of this exaltation – ἐκεῖνος ἐμὲ δοξάσει ("that one will glorify me," John 16:14) – the Spirit testifies of and witnesses of Christ – ἐκεῖνος μαρτυρήσει περὶ ἐμοῦ ("that one will testify concerning me," John 15:26). Thus, as "the Son submits to the Father's will in going to the cross . . . the Spirit's main ministry is to testify of Christ and point people toward him."[37] Relatedly, since "the very core of biblical faith" is "the cross of Christ,"[38] we recognize that Jesus sent the apostles into the world to be his witnesses (Matt 28:18–20; Luke 24:48; Acts 1:8). However, "*the chief witness* for Christ will be the Holy Spirit."[39] Because of this focus on Christ, "it is harder to perceive the distinct personality of the Spirit . . . partly because the Spirit is so successful in his work of focusing our attention on Jesus."[40] We might even say that it is "harder to perceive" the name of the Spirit since he points us to Christ.[41] His very identity is linked, then, with the exaltation of Christ.[42]

Equivalency between Christ and the Spirit

A second, potential reason for the lack of a name is the biblical "equivalency" between Christ and the Spirit. Other possible terms that describe this "equivalency" are "unity" or "bond." (It must be emphasized that this idea of equivalency is advanced while still maintaining the distinctness between the Spirit and the Son.) We note, for example, the titles of "the Spirit of Christ"

---

36. Horrell, "In the Name of the Father," 141. He also glorifies the Father: see John 16:13–15.
37. Feinberg, *No One Like Him*, 488.
38. Wright, *Mission of God*, 312.
39. Ferguson, *Holy Spirit*, 36, emphasis added.
40. Sanders, *Deep Things of God*, 154.
41. There is a related trajectory that could be explored. We are not called "Spiritians" but "Christians." The name of Christ gives us our identity. "At baptism [believers] receive the name of Christ and are brought under a new authority, baptized out of their own name, as it were, into Christ's name" (Ferguson, *Holy Spirit*, 146). A name for the Spirit might cause confusion as to our identity as *Christians*.
42. It is helpful to note the tangential issue of the Spirit *exalting the Father*: "Never is the first person *of* the third, but the other way around: 'the Spirit of God' (Gen 1:2; Matt 3:16), 'the Spirit of our God' (1 Cor 6:11), 'the Spirit of the living God' (2 Cor 3:3), 'the Spirit of the LORD' (Judg 3:10), and 'the Spirit of the Sovereign LORD' (Isa 61:1)" (Lewis and Demarest, *Integrative Theology*, 278).

(Rom 8:9; 1 Pet 1:11); "the Spirit of his Son" (Gal 4:6); "the Spirit of Jesus" (Acts 16:7); and "the Spirit of Jesus Christ" (Phil 1:19). David Tonghou Ngong concludes that "the Holy Spirit is understood to be the Spirit of Jesus Christ . . . the Holy Spirit is often conflated with Jesus Christ . . . the power in the name of Jesus is also the power of the Spirit."[43] Ferguson notes that "in Romans 8:9–10 . . . the Spirit and Christ are virtually interchangeable terms."[44] According to Hewett:

> In Rom 8:9–10 Paul uses the expressions "Spirit of God," "Spirit of Christ," and "Christ" as interchangeable. To "walk in the Spirit" is the same as "minding the things of the Spirit," which is the same as "being in the Spirit." All of these expressions are broadly synonymous with being "in Christ."[45]

In addition, Yves Congar summarizes the biblical evidence by stating that there can be "no Christology without pneumatology and no pneumatology without Christology."[46] As Samuel M. Ngewa points out concerning John 14:26: "The first point to remember is that the Holy Spirit will be sent in Jesus' name . . . which means that his will and that of Jesus are one."[47] Finally, "numerous New Testament Scriptures could be considered dyadic, because they link the Holy Spirit and the Son in common cause and activity."[48] These passages demonstrate some type of equivalency between Christ and the Spirit.

Relatedly, there is complete possession of the Spirit by Christ. First Corinthians 15:45 calls Christ "the last Adam, a life-giving spirit" (NIV). However, Ferguson contends that "the NIV translation may fail us, for 'spirit' in this context probably refers to the Holy Spirit, and should be capitalized."[49] Christ, then, is *the* "life-giving Spirit." Furthermore, "Christ on his ascension came into . . . complete possession of the Spirit . . . [and] . . . the resurrected Christ and the Spirit are one to us . . . [the Spirit] is *alter Christus*, another Christ, to us; ministerially he is indeed *allos paraklētos*."[50]

---

43. Tonghou Ngong, "Who is the Holy Spirit?," 314n.13.
44. Ferguson, *Holy Spirit*, 37.
45. Jewett, "Holy Spirit," 197.
46. Congar, *Word and the Spirit*, 1.
47. Ngewa, "John," 1310.
48. Leupp, *Knowing the Name of God*, 31–32. Examples given include Rom 1:4 and 1 Tim 3:16.
49. Ferguson, *Holy Spirit*, 54.
50. Ferguson, 54.

Thus, again, there is some type of oneness between Christ and the Spirit. In fact, the "Son and the Spirit are always together in carrying out the work of the Father."[51] If the name of the Spirit was given, this might diminish the equivalency between the Spirit and Christ, as well as this complete possession of the Spirit by Christ.[52] Again, by advancing this equivalency as well as possession, we need to be careful to maintain the distinction between them. The Spirit did not die for our sins. The Holy Spirit is *another* (different) comforter (John 14:26). We still maintain three distinct persons within one God.

The Spirit as the personal presence of Jesus is an additional example of this equivalency. This is most clearly seen in the book of Acts. The event of Pentecost presents us with an epochal event in the biblical trajectory of the Spirit. When "the Holy Spirit is poured out on Pentecost, his personal presence in salvation history after the finished work of Christ inaugurates a new era in God's ways with the world."[53] The dawning of a new era becomes pivotal – not the name of the Spirit. At Pentecost, "the Paraclete/Advocate is the Holy Spirit in a special role, namely as the personal presence of Jesus in the Christian while Jesus is with the Father."[54] An important phrase is found in John 14:17: ὅτι παρ' ὑμῖν μένει καὶ ἐν ὑμῖν ἔσται ("for he remains in you and will be in you"). Pentecost was "a Christological event,"[55] though we often assume it was merely a pneumatological event. Therefore, the disciples would have the Spirit "in" them after Pentecost, and not just "with" them as before. John Frame notes, "When the Spirit comes, inevitably Jesus comes with him and in him."[56] As further evidence of the foundational event of Pentecost coupled with the equivalency of the Spirit and Christ, we note Acts 2:33: "Exalted to the right hand of God, he has received from the Father the promised Holy Spirit and has poured out what you now see and hear." Christ *himself* poured out the Spirit

---

51. Sanders, *Deep Things of God*, 138–39. See also 2 Cor 3:17: "The Lord is the Spirit"; and Rev 3:1: ". . . him who holds the seven spirits of God" (or the Spirit in his fullness) (Ferguson, *Holy Spirit*, 54–56).

52. A potential corollary is found in the writings of John Owen, the Puritan author: ". . . whenever the Holy Spirit is mentioned, his relation to the Father and Son is included; for he is the Spirit of God" (Owen, *Discourse Concerning the Holy Spirit*, 35).

53. Sanders, *Deep Things of God*, 135.

54. Turner, "Holy Spirit," 349. Notice the curious use of the phrase "personal presence" in these last two authors cited.

55. See Ferguson, *Holy Spirit*, 79; cf. 107.

56. Frame, *Salvation Belongs to the Lord*, 34.

at Pentecost.⁵⁷ An additional clarification is given by author Migliore: "The work of the Spirit is *re-presentative*. It is the power of the Spirit that Christ is made present to believers. By re-presenting Christ – by bringing Christ into the present – the Spirit spans the gap between the then and there and the here and now."⁵⁸ What is a potential reason, then, for the lack of a name for the Holy Spirit? He is the personal presence of *Jesus*. Thus, we were already given a name. Adding an additional name (despite their equivalency) would be superfluous, distracting and possibly even confusing. The Spirit exalts Christ; the Spirit is equated with Christ (though still distinct from him). The final aspect of my proposal centers on the Spirit and his primary ministry.

Focus on His "Work" of Sanctification

The Spirit is the *Holy* Spirit. I believe that one purpose of this title is to spotlight his work of sanctification. As we saw above, Scripture mentions "the Spirit" more than two hundred times and "Holy Spirit" approximately ninety times.⁵⁹ What is the purpose of referring to him as the *Holy* Spirit? And not, for example, the "Loving Spirit" or the "Joyful Spirit"? Is he more holy than the Father or the Son? The answer is most certainly in the negative, for the holiness of the Father and the Son is clear – although not because of their titles/names.⁶⁰ Therefore, there must be a reason why the Spirit is consistently referred to as the *Holy* Spirit. (Often, familiarity lulls us into complacency. We have read the title of "the Holy Spirit" so many times that we may not pause to consider possible nuances to the phrase.) As evangelicals, we believe that "the Bible itself claims to be a testimony to the Triune God's activity and discourse in

---

57. The connection of this event with sanctification (covered below), is highlighted by James Nkansah-Obrempong. The "giving of the Spirit as an eschatological fulfillment opened the door for the believer to enter into the eschatological life or the end times. This eschatological hope motivates Christians to live holy and godly lives (2 Pet 3:11)" (Nkansah-Obrempong, *Foundations for African Theological Ethics*, 108). In addition, this dawning of the new era helps explain why the "blasphemy against the Holy Spirit" will not be forgiven. Such blasphemy would not *only* be "a personal reaction to Jesus, but a rejection of the Spirit's ministry and therefore of the evidence that the kingdom ha[d] come and the new age ha[d] dawned (*cf.* Mt. 12:25–29; Lk. 10:21)" (see Ferguson, *Holy Spirit*, 51).

58. Migliore, *Faith Seeking Understanding*, 227, emphasis by author.

59. Strong, *Enhanced Strong's Lexicon*, #4151.

60. John 17:11 is the only instance of the title "Holy Father" (though see Luke 11:2 and Rev 6:10). Israel was called to be קָדֹשׁ ("holy"), because the Lord was קָדֹשׁ ("holy") (Lev 11:44–45; 19:2; 20:7, 26; 21:8; Deut 7:6; 14:2; 26:19; 28:9). In fact, "holiness is the quintessential quality of Yahweh" (Hartley, *Leviticus*, 312). While no verse in Scripture contains the title "Holy Son," Jesus is called "the Holy One of God" in Mark 1:24; cf. Luke 1:35; Acts 3:14; 4:27, 30; Rev 3:7.

the world."⁶¹ Thus, we take seriously the words of the Holy Spirit and aim to discover their meaning. One nuance of these words could be a focus on this "work" of sanctification.

In Paul's Epistles, it is possible to see that each person of the Trinity has a dominant function attributed to him: The Father creates (1 Cor 8:6; 2 Cor 4:6; see also Gen 1:1; Isa 44:24; Mark 13:19); the Son redeems/saves (Rom 3:24; Eph 1:7; Titus 2:14; 3:6; see also 1 John 2:2); and the Spirit sanctifies/makes holy (Rom 15:16; 1 Cor 6:11; 2 Cor 3:18; 2 Thess 2:13). There may even be a chronological progression: the Father creates, the Son saves and the Spirit sanctifies. However, because of their same essence, they are united in their functions – the Son creates (John 1:3, 10; 1 Cor 8:6; Col 1:16); the Spirit creates (Job 33:4; Ps 33:6; 104:30); the Father redeems/saves (Rom 3:26; 2 Cor 5:18–19; Eph 2:4–5, 8; 1 Pet 1:3); the Spirit redeems/saves (John 3:5–6; Rom 8:4; 1 Cor 6:11; Titus 3:5); the Father sanctifies (Acts 15:9; Rom 8:29; Eph 1:3–4; 1 Thess 5:23; Heb 2:11; 10:10); and the Son sanctifies (1 Cor 1:2, 30; Eph 4:15–16; 5:25–27). Ferguson comments, "in the work of redemption which Christ spearheads, each person of the Trinity is engaged. The patristic maxim that all persons of the Trinity share in all external acts of God . . . is here (as in the resurrection) perfectly illustrated."⁶² Millard Erickson focuses more sharply: "Each of the three persons of the Trinity has had, for a period of time, a particular function unique to himself. This is to be understood as a temporary role for the purpose of accomplishing a given end, not a change in his status or essence."⁶³

Along with these functions "unique" to each person of the Trinity, there are other common characteristics and functions. For instance, all three have a part to play in the resurrection:

- Father – Acts 2:32; 17:31; Romans 8:11; 1 Corinthians 15:15; 1 Thessalonians 1:10;
- Son – John 2:19–21; 10:17–18;
- Spirit – John 6:63; Romans 1:4; 2 Corinthians 3:6; 1 Timothy 3:16; 1 Peter 3:18.

---

61. Brown, *Scripture as Communication*, 126.
62. Ferguson, *Holy Spirit*, 42–43.
63. Millard Erickson, *Introducing Christian Doctrine*, 103, quoted in Kunhiyop, *African Christian Ethics*, 52.

All three embody "truth":

- Father – Psalms 25:10; 31:5; 57:10; 86:15; 89:14; 119:160; John 17:3, 17; Romans 3:4;
- Son – John 1:14; 14:6; Ephesians 4:21; 1 John 5:20; Revelation 3:7; 19:11;
- Spirit – John 14:17; 15:26; 16:13; 1 John 5:6.

The complexity of our redemption by the "one true God in three persons" is evident with these examples. However, for our purposes, it is necessary to emphasize that the "primary" ministry of the Holy Spirit is to make us holy.[64] As we aim to live holy lives, then, we can be thankful that the "Holy Spirit plays an important role as the Agent of the moral life in biblical ethics."[65] We also note that while Jesus Christ is the "model" for Christian ethics, the Holy Spirit is the "power" for Christian ethics.[66] Living an ethical life is the result of the work of sanctification by the Holy Spirit.

The biblical terms for "sanctify" or "make holy" convey the idea of separation.[67] This idea of separation could be an additional nuance to the title of the Holy Spirit, for it may be used to distinguish the Holy Spirit from other spirits – he is completely separate, wholly different from them. He is, indeed, the *Holy* Spirit.[68] The mention of a (different) name would not allow for this important nuance. The Spirit is not like the numerous other spirits. He is distinct, holy and separate. This idea gains traction when we note that the ancient world was much more cognizant of the role of the spirit world in

---

64. It is worth noting that all members of the Africa Society of Evangelical Theology sign the Statement of Faith, which includes Article V, #4: "The Spirit applies the salvation won by Christ by regenerating and sanctifying believers who respond to God's grace."

65. Nkansah-Obrempong, *Foundations for African Theological Ethics*, 106.

66. See Kunhiyop, *African Christian Ethics*, 53–54. This reality reminds us of the opaqueness surrounding the Spirit. While "model" implies a person, "power" in this context is impersonal. Yet, just because the Spirit is paired with "impersonal things" (as we saw above in the words of the Jehovah's Witnesses) or described as the "power" for Christian ethics, this does not negate his personhood. The Jehovah's Witnesses are guilty here of an "either/or" perspective, rather than a correct "both/and" way of thinking. The Holy Spirit is the "power," *and* he is a person.

67. Ferguson, *Holy Spirit*, 140.

68. See Owen, *Discourse Concerning the Holy Spirit*, 36.

everyday lives.[69] This awareness of the spirit world is true of many societies in Africa.[70]

The passage of 1 Corinthians 6:11 further explicates this work by the Spirit, "you were washed, you were sanctified, you were justified in the name of the Lord Jesus Christ and by the Spirit of our God." This verse is central to my proposal: we are sanctified by the Spirit, but in the name of Christ. If we were given the Spirit's name, this possibly would be confusing ("Into which name are we washed, sanctified and justified?"). However, there is no confusion – we are sanctified into the name of Christ and by the Spirit. The words of Ferguson pick up on the Spirit's work, as well as echo our previous assertion of the equivalency between Christ and the Spirit: "The goal of [the Spirits'] activity is transformation into the likeness of Christ (Rom 8:29). In a word, for the New Testament, sanctification, or holiness, is Christlikeness."[71]

Every time we read the title of "the *Holy* Spirit," then, we are to notice the adjective "Holy," and then reflect on the primary work of the Spirit. If the name of the Spirit was mentioned, this could *possibly* hinder our progression in sanctification. We are called to "make every effort . . . to be holy" (Heb 12:14), and we all need consistent reminders to pursue this holiness. The phrase of "the Holy Spirit" could very well be one such reminder.

Before concluding, it is worth noting two other ideas that (1) require more investigation and (2) might illuminate the reason for the lack of a name for the Holy Spirit. The first relates to the doctrine of the "procession" of the Spirit. The Cappadocian father Gregory of Nyssa wrote: "The Father's property is unbegottenness or the property of being ungenerate (*agennēsia*). The Son's characteristic is begottenness (*gennasia*), and the Spirit's is mission or procession (*ekpempsis, ekporeusis*)."[72] Ferguson points out that the Son sends the Spirit from the Father, yet the Spirit proceeds or "goes out" (*ekporeuomai*) from the Father (John 15:26). He continues

> a clear distinction in tenses is evident in these words: Jesus *will send* (*pempsō*, future tense); the Spirit *proceeds* (*ekporeuomai*,

---

69. "The Israelites believed in a universe that was common among the civilizations of the biblical world. It encompassed three parts: *a heavenly realm*, an earthly realm for humans, and an underworld for the dead" (Heiser, *I Dare You*, 3, emphasis added).

70. On the African continent there is "much interest in the spirit world," as well as a "spiritual worldview," in contrast to a Western "scientific worldview" (Gwamna, *Perspectives in African Theology*, Kindle edition, 13–14).

71. Ferguson, *Holy Spirit*, 139.

72. See Cornelius Plantinga, Jr., "Gregory of Nyssa and the Social Analogy of the Trinity," *The Thomist* 50 (July 1986): 330–31, quoted in Feinberg, *No One Like Him*, 483.

present continuous tense) ... The sending is a specific future event (and is fulfilled at Pentecost); the proceeding, however, appears to be constantly true of the Spirit. It is his nature to proceed from the Father.[73]

Jewett writes that this procession describes "the essential nature of the Spirit himself, that is, it is an 'ontological' clause. The Holy Spirit is the One who eternally proceeds from the Father."[74] Thus, possibly his identity is not summarized or reflected in a name but rather in his procession from the Father. The second idea concerns the Spirit as the uniting bond between the Father and the Son. Sanders echoes this argument attributed to Augustine, "The love between [the Father and the Son] is itself a full, distinct, subsistent person. The eternal love going on within the Trinity is like a complex life, or a drama, or a dance, and it is personified in the Holy Spirit."[75] Also C. S. Lewis, "The union between the Father and the Son is such a live concrete thing that this union itself is also a Person."[76] Thus, it is possible to speculate that for some thinkers, no name was given because the Spirit is the bond of love between the Father and the Son.

Conclusion

There is much evidence for "the rich tapestry of the Spirit's work."[77] Yet, there seems to remain an opaqueness concerning his name. While some believe that "Holy Spirit" is his name, we have seen possible reasons to question this assertion. As a way of conclusion, I propose an analogy that will help me illustrate not only the total misunderstanding by the Jehovah's Witnesses as it concerns this topic, but also their complete neglect in acknowledging the complexity of the issue. The Church of Jesus Christ of Latter-day Saints, otherwise known as the Mormons, frequently quote a passage from the book of Amos: "Surely the Lord GOD will do nothing, But he revealeth his secret unto his servants the prophets" (Amos 3:7 KJV). Several Mormon sources interpret

---

73. Ferguson, *Holy Spirit*, 76.
74. Jewett, "Holy Spirit," 201.
75. Sanders, *Deep Things of God*, 233; cf. Augustine of Hippo, "On the Holy Trinity," 15.17.27, 29 (NPNF 1/3:215–16).
76. C. S. Lewis, *Mere Christianity*, 152, quoted in Sanders, *Deep Things of God*, 233.
77. Ferguson, *Holy Spirit*, 147.

this passage as a defense of modern-day, Mormon prophetic authority.[78] They claim that the true church of Jesus Christ will be led by prophets. However, they exhibit a complete lack of understanding of the work of the Spirit. Ferguson notes that because of the Spirit's work, Christians receive an anointing

> which results in their knowing the truth (1 John 2:20). They do not need anyone to teach them (1 John 2:27). Now, in Christ, all believers share in his anointing with the Spirit and have knowledge of the Lord without human mediation, in distinction from old covenant knowledge of God which was mediated through prophets, priests and kings.[79]

Thus, there is a fundamental lack of understanding in the Mormon church of a crucial development in the biblical witness. All believers enjoy knowledge of the Triune God, and are not dependent on prophets to guide them. However, the Mormons ignore this reality.[80] In a similar fashion, the Jehovah's Witnesses ignore extensive biblical evidence concerning the Holy Spirit, much of which gives plausible reasons for the apparent lack of a "name" for the Holy Spirit.[81] A superficial interpretation of Amos 3:7 results in the Mormon interpretation of the need for modern-day prophets. Relatedly, a simplistic and superficial conclusion on the part of the Jehovah's Witnesses, that is "there is no name for the Holy Spirit," results in a complete lack of understanding of the full witness of Scripture. It is possible that the identity of the Holy Spirit is not explained or illustrated through his name. Rather, as I have attempted to argue, his identity as the third person of the Trinity is centered on exalting Christ, on the equivalency between himself and Christ and to emphasize his main ministry of sanctifying the people of God.

---

78. For example, see Church of Jesus Christ of Latter-day Saints, *New Testament Seminary Teacher*, 13; Church of Jesus Christ of Latter-day Saints, *Primary 5*, 7.

79. Ferguson, *Holy Spirit*, 121.

80. And yet, with an apparent contradictory stance, the Mormon church also maintains "considerable leeway for *individual* scriptural evaluation" (Givens and Barlow, *Oxford Handbook on Mormonism*, 127, emphasis added).

81. In addition, they ignore over fifty passages in the NT where the three persons of the Trinity are mentioned together: Matt 1:18–23; 4:1–10; 12:28; 28:19; Mark 1:10–11; 12:35–37; Luke 1:35; 4:18; John 1:32–34; 3:34–35; 14:16–17, 26; 15:26; 16:13–15; Acts 1:4–5; 2:33; 7:48–52; 10:38; 20:21–24; Rom 1:1–4; 5:5–6; 8:1–4, 9, 13–17; 15:16, 17–19, 30; 1 Cor 2:10–16; 6:11; 12:4–6; 2 Cor 1:21–22; 13:14; Gal 3:11–14; 4:4–6; 5:21–24; Eph 1:3–14; 2:18, 22; 3:4–7, 14–17; 4:4–6; 5:18–20; 1 Thess 5:18–19; 2 Thess 2:13–14; 1 Tim 3:15–16; Titus 3:4–6; Heb 9:14; 10:29–30; 1 Pet 1:2; 3:18; 1 John 3:23–24; 4:2; 5:6–9; Jude 20–21.

Bibliography

Ambrose of Milan. "Three Books of St. Ambrose on the Holy Spirit." In *St. Ambrose: Select Works and Letters*. Translated by H. de Romestin, E. de Romestin, and H. T. F. Duckworth. In vol. 10 of *The Nicene and Post-Nicene Fathers*, Second Series. Edited by Philip Schaff and Henry Wace. New York: Christian Literature Company, 1896.

Assohoto, Barnabé. "Genesis." In *Africa Bible Commentary*, edited by Tokunboh Adeyemo, 9–84. Nairobi, Kenya: WordAlive; Grand Rapids: Zondervan, 2006.

Augustine of Hippo. "On the Trinity." In *St. Augustin: On the Holy Trinity, Doctrinal Treatises, Moral Treatises*. Translated by Arthur West Haddan. In *The Nicene and Post-Nicene Fathers*, First Series. Edited by Philip Schaff. Buffalo, NY: Christian Literature Company, 1887.

Brown, Jeannine K. *Scripture as Communication: Introducing Biblical Hermeneutics*. Grand Rapids, MI: Baker Academic, 2007.

Calvin, John. *Institutes of the Christian Religion*. Vol 1. Bellingham: Logos Bible Software, 1997.

Church of Jesus Christ of Latter-day Saints. *New Testament Seminary Teacher Resource Manual*. Salt Lake City, UT: The Church of Jesus Christ of Latter-day Saints, 1999.

———. *Primary 5: Doctrine and Covenants; Church History, Ages 8–11*. Vol. 2. Salt Lake City: Church of Jesus Christ of Latter-day Saints, 1996.

Congar, Yves. *The Word and the Spirit*. San Francisco: Harper & Row, 1986.

Enns, Paul P. *The Moody Handbook of Theology*. Chicago: Moody Press, 1989.

Feinberg, John S. *No One Like Him: The Doctrine of God*. Wheaton: Crossway, 2001.

Ferguson, Sinclair B. *The Holy Spirit*. Downers Grove: InterVarsity Press, 1996.

Frame, John M. *Salvation Belongs to the Lord: An Introduction to Systematic Theology*. Phillipsburg, NJ: P&R Publishing, 2006.

Givens, Terryl L., and Philip L. Barlow, eds. *Oxford Handbook on Mormonism*. Oxford: Oxford University Press, 2015.

Gwamna, Je'adayibe Dogara. *Perspectives in African Theology: Volume Two*. Jos: Africa Christian Textbooks, 2014. Kindle Edition.

Hartley, John E. *Leviticus*. Word Biblical Commentary 4. Dallas, TX: Word, 1992.

Hawthorne, Gerald F. "Holy Spirit." In *Dictionary of the Later New Testament and Its Developments*, edited by Ralph P. Martin and Peter H. Davids, 489–99. Downers Grove, IL: InterVarsity Press, 1997.

Heiser, Michael S. *I Dare You Not to Bore Me with the Bible*. Bellingham, WA: Lexham Press, 2014.

Horrell, J. Scott. "In the Name of the Father, Son and Holy Spirit: Toward a Trinitarian Worldview." *Bibliotheca Sacra* 166 (April-June 2009): 131–46.

Jewett, P. K. "Holy Spirit." In *The Zondervan Encyclopedia of the Bible*, vol. 3, H–L, edited by Moisés Silva and Merrill Chapin Tenney, 192–209. Grand Rapids, MI: Zondervan, 2009.

Keener, Craig S. *The IVP Bible Background Commentary: New Testament*. 2nd ed. Downers Grove, IL: IVP Academic, 2014.
Kunhiyop, Samuel Waje. *African Christian Ethics*. Grand Rapids, MI: Zondervan, 2008.
Leupp, Roderick T. *Knowing the Name of God: A Trinitarian Tapestry of Grace, Faith and Community*. Downers Grove, IL: InterVarsity Press, 1996.
Lewis, Gordon R., and Bruce A. Demarest. *Integrative Theology, vol. 1, Knowing Ultimate Reality – The Living God*. Grand Rapids, MI: Zondervan, 1987.
Migliore, Daniel L. *Faith Seeking Understanding: An Introduction to Christian Theology*. 2nd ed. Grand Rapids, MI: Eerdmans, 2004.
Nestle, Eberhard et al. *The Greek New Testament*, 27th ed. Stuttgart: Deutsche Bibelgesellschaft, 1993.
Ngewa, Samuel M. "John." In *Africa Bible Commentary*, edited by Tokunboh Adeyemo, 1277–322. Nairobi, Kenya: WordAlive; Grand Rapids, MI: Zondervan, 2006.
Nkansah-Obrempong, James. *Foundations for African Theological Ethics*. Carlisle, Cumbria: Langham Monographs, 2013.
O'Collins, Gerald. *The Tripersonal God: Understanding and Interpreting the Trinity*. New York: Paulist Press, 1999.
Owen, John. *A Discourse Concerning the Holy Spirit*. Philadelphia: Presbyterian Board of Publication, n.d.
Sanders, Fred. *The Deep Things of God: How the Trinity Changes Everything*. Wheaton, IL: Crossway, 2010.
Smith, Jerome H. *The New Treasury of Scripture Knowledge*. Nashville, TN: Nelson, 1992.
Strong, James. *Enhanced Strong's Lexicon*. n.p.: Woodside Bible Fellowship, 1995.
Tonghou Ngong, David. "Who Is the Holy Spirit in Contemporary African Christianity?" In *Majority World Theology: Christian Doctrine in Global Context*, edited by Gene L. Green, Stephen T. Pardue, and K. K. Yeo, 310–22. Downers Grove, IL: InterVarsity Press, 2020.
Torrey, R. A. *The Person and Work of the Holy Spirit as Revealed in the Scriptures and in Personal Experience*. New York: Revell, 1910.
Turner, M. M. B. "Holy Spirit." In *Dictionary of Jesus and the Gospels*, edited by Joel B. Green, Scot McKnight, and I. Howard Marshall, 341–51. Downers Grove, IL: InterVarsity Press, 1992.
Watchtower Bible and Tract Society. "Jehovah's Witnesses Around the World." *JW.org*, About Us. https://www.jw.org/en/jehovahs-witnesses/worldwide.
———. *Holy Spirit – The Force Behind the Coming New Order!* Brooklyn, NY: Watchtower Bible and Tract Society, 1976.
———. *Reasoning from the Scriptures*. Brooklyn, NY: Watchtower Bible and Tract Society, 1985.
———. *Should You Believe in the Trinity?* Brooklyn, NY: Watchtower Bible and Tract Society, 1989.

———. "What Is the Holy Spirit?" *JW.org*, Bible Teachings, Bible Questions Answered. https://www.jw.org/en/bible-teachings/questions/what-is-the-holy-spirit/.

Wood, A. S. "Holiness." In *The Zondervan Encyclopedia of the Bible*, vol. 3, H–L, edited by Moisés Silva and Merrill Chapin Tenney, 179–91. Grand Rapids, MI: Zondervan, 2009.

Wright, Christopher J. H. *The Mission of God*. Nottingham: Inter-Varsity Press, 2006.

6

"I Banged the Table Three Times"

The Empowering Spirit and Women in the AINC

Esther Mombo
Professor, St. Paul's University, Limuru, Kenya

and

Heleen Joziasse
Diaconial worker with Stek (voor Stad en Kerk), Protestant Church in The Hague, The Netherlands

Abstract

It has been argued that the neglect of the Spirit in the Christian theological tradition bears some direct relation to the repression and marginalization of women in the churches. African Instituted Churches (AICs) however, have been known for their emphasis on the Holy Spirit and power. It appears that women in these churches share in the power of the Spirit and subvert patriarchal and colonial norms, which are deeply rooted in both mission churches as well as in AICs, even when women are founders of some of these churches.[1] This is for instance visible in leadership structures, issues of authority and

---

1. See the examples of women's leadership in AICs in Mwaura, "Gender and Power in African Christianity," 422–29, 438–45. An example of a woman founder of an AIC negotiating male hierarchy is given in Kgatle, "Remarkable Woman." See also Hinga, "Women, Power and Liberation."

lines of succession. This paper seeks to show and evaluate how women in the African Israel Nineveh Church (AINC), through the manifestation of the Holy Spirit, are affirmed in their equal human dignity and how through the power of the Holy Spirit these women are enabled to raise their voice, claim space and build the church as a community of equals. The paper will use a narrative methodology to bring to the fore the women's voices, articulating their perspectives on pneumatology.[2]

Key words: pneumatology, African women's theologies, AINC, African Instituted Churches, leadership, postcolonial, gender

Introduction: Narrative Methodology

When discussing the manifestation of the Spirit in African Christian communities and the relation between pneumatology and community, it needs to be clear which Christian community is being discussed, and who is allowed to reason and articulate theology in this community. Again, when we argue that in an African pneumatology the experiences of the power of the Holy Spirit are fundamental, it is important to discern *whose* experiences with the Holy Spirit are regarded and acknowledged. In this article we explore the contours of the pneumatology as explicated by women from the AINC. The methodology for writing this paper is derived from the Circle of Concerned African Women Theologians, using a narrative epistemology. In African women's theologies the narrative methodology is used to explore and bring to the fore the faith experiences of women and to add new (female) insights to theological reflection in order to attain a relevant and holistic theology. Narratives, in an expression of Sarojini Nadar, are perceived as data with soul.[3] In African women's theologies these data are brought into dialogue with the Bible in order to bring out new insights about the Triune God in relation to the human community. Hence, the theology of the Holy Spirit according to women in the AINC (and AICs in general) emerges, not from written accounts but from their lived experiences. Prior to listening to the voices of women in the AINC, which is one of the prominent AICs in Kenya, we will explore the intersection of pneumatology and gender from different angles. Following the

---

2. The citations in this article are derived from an extensive collaborative research of the authors of this article, focused on Christology and gender relations in the AINC and the RCEA, conducted between 2013 and 2018. See Joziasse, "Women's Faith Seeking Life."

3. Nadar, "'Stories Are Data with Soul,'" 18–28.

story of one AINC/woman, Caren, the various insights on pneumatology from the perspective of women in the AINC will be discussed.

Pneumatology and Gender

In the Christian tradition God is confessed through the triune revelation of God, Jesus Christ (his life, death and resurrection) and the Holy Spirit. The Spirit, as the Paraclete, consoles Christians in the midst of life struggles and challenges Christians to give prophetic witness to the God of love. The third article of the Nicene Creed therefore affirms that God is not only *over* and *for* us but also at work *in* us; the new humanity in Christ is articulated.[4] This immanent character of the Holy Spirit could account for the negligence or suspicion with which the Spirit is approached in theological treatises. Thus, Daniel Migliore argues that movements in history that stressed the presence and power of the Spirit were met with opposition by the institutional church "that looked on the experience of and appeal to the Spirit as potentially subversive and in need of control."[5] Other scholars have shown that in the early church particularly the spirit-filled movements appeared to be attractive to women, offering them a more equal space in the church and its leadership.[6] Hence, it seems that the exclusion of women from official leadership in the churches and little elaborated pneumatology went hand in hand.

Women theologians in the Minority World gave discussions on pneumatology an important impetus by critiquing the depiction of the divine Trinity in exclusively male terms and symbols. While the first two persons in the Trinity are referred to with explicitly male designations such as Lord, Father and Son, the Holy Spirit is ambiguous where gender is concerned. The Spirit has been referred to in female terminology, pointing at the gender of the Hebrew word *ruach* as feminine while in Greek the Spirit is indicated with the grammatically neuter *pneuma*.[7] Moreover, the early church fathers Theophilus of Antioch and Irenaeus equated the Holy Spirit with the wisdom of God, Sophia. Nicole Slee therefore argues "these central biblical metaphors for the Spirit offer support for the notion of a feminine Spirit which, though

---

4. Migliore, *Faith Seeking Understanding*, 223.

5. Migliore, 224.

6. Torjesen, *When Women Were Priests*; Clark, *Women in the Early Church*; Madigan and Osiek, *Ordained Women in the Early Church*; Taylor and Ramelli, *Patterns of Women's Leadership*.

7. In Latin, the language of the Roman Empire, the official language of the Roman Catholic Church from the fourth century onwards, the grammatical gender of the word "Spiritus" is masculine.

largely repressed in Christian tradition, has nevertheless persisted."[8] While the Holy Spirit can be regarded in feminine imagery, for instance in the image of a kind mother, others have voiced the concern that this would reduce women's identity to the role of mothering and reinforce the patriarchal concept of God by adding "femininity" while at the same time affirming male superiority.[9] Therefore, instead of focusing on discussions about pneumatology in relation to the gender of God, women theologians (in the Minority and Majority World) have turned to explicating pneumatology as the expression of divine immanence; the Spirit of God is present and at work in the world through matter, bodies and, in fact, also through women.[10] Hence, pneumatology is a vehicle for women (as it is for men), not only to embody, but also to express and theologize how human beings participate in the creating and sustaining presence of God in this world.

Pneumatology in African Instituted Churches

Since the concept of God was transposed wholesale into African theology, pneumatology remained for a long time a fairly unchartered area, particularly in theologies affiliated with mission churches. Yet, as Allan Anderson has pointed out, particularly in the churches of the Spirit, which account for a large part of the African Initiated Churches (AICs), an incarnated grassroots theology developed, addressing the theological vacuum.

> This is theology from the underside, a people's theology. These churches have made possible a dialogue between the African thought world and Christianity at an existential level. Theology based on a European model has missed much in biblical pneumatology that speaks directly into the world of Africa – and in fact into the worldview of almost everyone except Western peoples.[11]

Anderson signals that the "Spirit" or "wind" is that which a person receives from God and is a shared feature with the divine. The Spirit grants being and life, strength and power, harmonizing a person with the rest of humanity and the universe. In the Bible the presence of the Spirit is often linked to the gift

---

8. Slee, "Holy Spirit and Spirituality," 171.
9. See Clifford, *Introducing Feminist Theology*, 110.
10. Stephenson, "Where the Wind Blows," 330.
11. Anderson, "African Initiated Churches," 179.

of leadership, whereas leadership is vested in power which has its source in the Spirit. Similarly, prophesy, healing and declaring the word of God through the Spirit are important gifts bestowed on both men and women.[12] Important biblical references supporting the role of women through the Spirit are Acts 2:17–18, about the Spirit enabling women to prophesy, and 1 Corinthians 12:7–11, 27–31 referring to the gifts of the Spirit being distributed irrespective of gender, including the gift of apostleship.[13] The biblical concept of power that is sought and claimed through the Holy Spirit, according to Anderson, is similar to the notion of "power" in Africa, conveying "forcefulness, strength and ability. It carries with it the idea of dignity, authority and power over oppression. It also refers to power in action and has its ultimate source in God."[14] Against the accusations of syncretism and mingling with pre-Christian expressions he holds that "unusual" manifestations of the Spirit were experienced both in biblical as well as in recent times, for instance in AICs, and "must be accepted as genuine responses to the working of the Spirit among ordinary African people."[15]

The power of the Spirit liberates from the oppression of both the spirit world and Western colonial forms of Christianity, and – as African women theologians emphasize – the Spirit liberates women from dehumanization and gender injustice. In the next section we will further focus on the meaning of the Spirit for women in AICs.

The Spirit and Women in the AINC

It is from the centrality of the Holy Spirit in the AICs of the Spirit-type, and the lived realities of women in these churches, that African women theologians link "the AICs' pneumatology with liberative anthropology that undergirds gender justice in leadership and exercising gifts of the Holy Spirit."[16] Philomena Mwaura for instance emphasizes that in AICs, women – particularly women

---

12. Anderson, 181.
13. Rom 16:7; cf. 1 Cor 12:28–29.
14. Anderson, "African Initiated Churches," 180.
15. Sometimes there may be play-acting and manipulation through a bogus "manifestation of the Spirit" – but Christianity throughout the world has false prophets and people using religious sanctions to enforce their own will. . . . If charges of "syncretism" are levelled at African Spirit churches, then the same criteria must be used for churches in the Western world that have unconsciously absorbed elements of the surrounding secular, materialistic, postmodern culture and worldview.
Anderson, 186.
16. Phiri and Kaunda, "African Instituted Churches," 6.

in liminal positions – receive power and have leadership roles, whereas in missionary churches women predominantly fill the pews.[17] Since the Holy Spirit is perceived as the power endowed on all believers, cutting across sociocultural, gender, age and race hierarchies, pneumatology brings forward the mediation of enabling power to lead, preach, prophesy, exorcise, heal, dream and see visions, to women and men equally.

Life stories of women in the AINC further reveal how in their lived realities, and through their experiences of the Holy Spirit, they receive agency and subjectivity. It appears that the Spirit of Jesus empowers women to resist and subvert unjust relations of power in church and in society, as an expression of a broader, holistic life-giving power.[18] AINC women attest to the Holy Spirit as a truly life-giving power, proclaimed by Jesus Christ – "I have come that they may have life and have it to the full" (John 10:10). In this light we will further explore the meaning of the Holy Spirit for women in the AINC. The AINC is a Spirit-type AIC that was founded by John Kivuli in 1941 in Nineveh, a place in Western Kenya not far from Kisumu.[19] The name *African* refers to "an African person, black in color" and its leadership,[20] while the name *Israel* reflects the notion of being a chosen people. The name *Nineveh* points at the centrality of confession and repentance in the liturgy and in the lived faith experiences of the members of this church. All members, irrespective of age, wear white tunics and a white scarf (women) or cap (men), symbolizing the discipleship of equals. Between 1974 and 1983 the AINC was led by the widow of Kivuli, High Priest Mama Rebecca.

The following story was narrated by Caren while seated in a small church office of the AINC. The story is situated in a time when Caren was not yet a member of the AINC. Raised in a Roman Catholic home, as a young woman Caren was raped by a doctor and had to become the wife of her abuser. Since her husband developed an alcohol addiction Caren started to attend to patients herself with prayer, using holy water and oil. As a result, many people came for healing to her, instead of to her husband, the doctor. Because of her healing gifts, she was sent away to her parents-in-law where she was appointed as lay coordinator in a local parish in a mission area of the Roman Catholic Church. There, she pushed for the construction of a church building, instead of using

---

17. Mwaura, "Gender and Power in African Christianity," 410–45.
18. Phiri and Kaunda, "African Instituted Churches," 7.
19. See Kudoyi, "African Israel Nineveh Church"; Welbourn and Ogot, *Place to Feel at Home*; Kivuli, "Modernization of an African Independent Church," 58–68.
20. African Israel Nineveh Church, "Sheria za African Israel Nineveh Church," 3.

the school premises. Caren recalls how during a meeting that was organized "to build the hearts of the parishioners in preparation of building a new church," God took her out from the Catholic church.

> So when we started, the first item on the agenda was raised by the father who said: "From today I don't want sinners to be taken away from church, without taking them to me first. You should tell me what you have done, so that I can judge whether you have sinned or not." In the Catholic church sometimes we have many people, but sometimes we don't have many people, we miss them. Especially in December when people are supposed to come for Christmas, when we wait for Jesus to be born, many people enter sinning. They do sin, they get pregnant and the ladies and the men leave the church, and thus during that time we don't have many people in the churches.
>
> After the father had spoken, I was very harsh, I don't know what came to me. I asked: "Why should you tell us that people have to come to you? When Adam and Eve made a mistake in the Garden of Eden, did God go there to tell them that they have sinned? They themselves saw the sin and they went to hide themselves. So, you cannot ask people to come to you to tell their sins and to judge whether they can stay in the church or not." And the catechist told me, "Caren, you can't say that, because the missionaries went to be trained so that they can interpret the Bible in the right way. You don't know, you translate the Bible in your own way." So I stood, that time, I stood up and banged the table three times and said, "This is not the time to be taught by a human being, but this is the time to be taught by the Holy Spirit." So I took my notes and went out and I was the one who had started the meeting.
>
> I went outside for some minutes and as I was going, I heard a voice and ever since I was born I had not heard a voice: "Caren, look up!" And I looked up and I saw a cloud of fire coming down. And I understood: if you dare to go back to this church, this fire will burn you. And I fell down, you know the voice of God . . . I fell there, I was unconscious. I don't know how long I stayed like that, but then I could see. And I sat down and after sitting down I stood up. Just when I stood up, a leader came out from the church,

my neighbor, and she told me, "Even me, I have seen this meeting is not good. Let's go home."[21]

From this story we can derive various insights regarding African women's pneumatology as expressed by an AINC woman. First, in this testimony Caren narrates how the Spirit, perceived as power of God, took possession over her. Apparently, apart from speech or words, the Spirit is mediated through signs such as a voice, fire, bright light and physical signs (falling, shaking). These are experienced as expressions of divine presence: God immanent in the daily life and actively involved in and through a woman. It is this Spirit – present in various manifestations – that grants Caren authority to raise her voice. Hence, this story of Caren illustrates what Phiri and Kaunda in their research of the lived faith experiences among members of AICs in Southern Africa, have identified: women perceive God, the God of the Bible, as the ultimate bestower of authority. They hold that it is God through the Holy Spirit who decides who would be empowered for manifestation of the Holy Spirit and leadership.[22]

Moreover, the story of Caren reveals that the authority of the Spirit is entrusted to her by God to raise her voice and speak out. She bases her acts and words on the interventions of the Holy or divine Spirit. As a prayer healer, prophetess and preacher, Caren channels the Holy Spirit at work among people. This empowerment by the Holy Spirit is irrespective of education or marital status. In the AINC (the church Caren later joined) as in many other Spirit churches,[23] the power of the Spirit is not preserved for the chosen few; it is not coupled to hierarchy, office or gender. In the AINC on the eighth day, newborn babies are baptized with the Spirit and receive spiritual gifts.[24] Hence, every human being is enabled to invoke or mediate the Holy Spirit.

Similar to other Spirit churches, the AINC can be viewed as a community of pneumatics, the various gifts of the Spirit are acknowledged and valued. The Holy Spirit is at the center of the lived Christology of women – Jesus saves through the Spirit – and pneumatology is at the center of ecclesiology and liturgy.[25] AINC women like Caren, receive visions and dreams, they foresee events, give advice, prevent people from going astray and they get the power

---

21. AINC Interview 15 Caren, Ruiru: 5-3-2014.
22. Phiri and Kaunda, "African Instituted Churches."
23. Hinga, "Women, Power and Liberation," 281–82.
24. Joziasse, "Women's Faith Seeking Life," 157.
25. Joziasse, 232.

to heal.[26] Since women (in theory) equally partake in these gifts of the Spirit, they are empowered, receive authority, are agents and bear knowledge of the Spirit and the working of the Spirit. The Spirit grants women agency. The Holy Spirit moved Caren to raise her voice against abuse of power (the Roman Catholic priest who seizes the power to morally judge his congregants). The banging of the table thrice is a sign of authority and power. It is both culturally and religiously a subversive act: women are not supposed to raise their voice publicly, nor to reinforce their words through loud noise. Hence, both the gender hierarchy as well as ecclesial hierarchy are challenged.

Being Set Free

Apart from emphasizing the social and political implications of this pneumatology for the liberation of women, focused on leadership roles within the AICs, as convincingly have been pointed out by African women theologians, it should be first and foremost noted that AINC women formulate the state of being filled by the Holy Spirit in terms of receiving a new identity, or being set free. Women experience the Spirit as a source of dignity and respect. The power of the Holy Spirit frees women of barriers imposed on them, be they religious, cultural, economic or racial. In this respect AINC women often speak of receiving a new name.[27] With the expression "Jesus gave me a new name"[28] women indicate they are granted a new identity and their status is uplifted. One AINC woman explains this in the following way:

> Earlier on people of my clan despised and looked down upon me, but today they respect me because God has given me a new name. In general the community has a low opinion about women. However, for me by now I am respected because I can be consulted for decision-making and I can also offer support to people in need. I really matter in the community because I do these things.[29]

---

26. In AINC Interview 13 Joyce, Ruiru: 11-12-2014, Joyce narrates that more and more people came to her house for healing; she prayed for barren women who got pregnant and afterwards she dedicated the babies to God.

27. Joziasse, "Women's Faith Seeking Life," 232.

28. Joziasse, 200.

29. AINC Interview 9 Elisabeth, Kendu Bay: 13-4-2014. Hinga in her study of the Legio Maria Church points at the "symbolic status reversal" – people who are in reality without a public position or of low status, receive symbolic status through participating in a hierarchy in which everybody has a position and through the creation of a headquarters with an administrative center. Hinga, "Women, Power and Liberation," 206–10.

This pneumatology is anchored in the salvation history of Jesus Christ as revealed in the word of God (the Bible) that implies that women who are filled with the Holy Spirit, just like men, are empowered to take part in the life giving and saving mission of Jesus. Women become channels of divine power, as expressed in this quotation: "God uses women a lot in the AINC to help people in the church. Women help for instance in family issues, they receive the Holy Spirit who reveals the hidden agendas and their testimonies are used to bring people to church."[30] Hence, the endowment with the Holy Spirit for women is drawn toward bringing people to the church, which is perceived as the embodiment of Jesus Christ, and living a good, morally uplifted life. In the narrative of Caren the morality and "the good life" is at stake; she challenges the priest's authority to define and to forgive sin.

Life-Giving Spirit

Women in Spirit churches perceive the Holy Spirit as the life-giving spirit who restores life and harmony and establishes right relations. This is distinct from evil spirits who are there to destroy, to kill and to fight. The intervention of Caren through the Holy Spirit was directed toward restoring harmony and right relation in the community. Similarly, in her research of the Legio Maria Church, Teresia Hinga has pointed at the central meaning of the Holy Spirit in terms of liberating from evil, personified in Satan or evil spirits.[31] The Holy Spirit is perceived as a weapon in the battle against evil spirits and against the effects that these spirits have in the human realm, for example mental illness, all kinds of somatic disorders and bareness, but also accidents, theft, addiction, dispute and discrimination or social and political disorder. The Holy Spirit is identified as the life-giving Spirit in which Christians participate; women are actors through their spiritual gifts. It is from this life-giving power that Caren narrates how she got out of the Catholic church, which to her was an oppressive place where the Spirit was not at work.

AINC women narrate that salvation through Jesus implies that they have been set free by his Spirit.[32] One of the consequences of being set free, as formulated by women in the AINC, is that this Spirit-filled state not only liberates women from "old" cultural, religious and economic identities and from evil or Satan, but the Holy Spirit and the gifts of the Spirit also put them

---

30. AINC Interview 1 Esther, Ruiru: 6-3-2014.
31. Hinga, "Women, Power and Liberation," 288.
32. Joziasse, "Women's Faith Seeking Life," 201.

in a new relation to men: "the Holy Spirit has set people free to regard men and women as equal."[33] The Holy Spirit effects an egalitarian ethos and appears to enhance the liberation of women from patriarchal oppression and hierarchy in ecclesiological structures (also) within Spirit-oriented AICs.[34] Hinga argues that in the Legio Maria Church, a Spirit church in Western Kenya, which broke away from the Roman Catholic Church,

> the belief that the Holy Spirit is a power that impartially and compellingly grips people from without, and empowers them, enables individuals who would otherwise be mute and indifferent and hence unable to articulate their views, to do so. According to them, the Holy Spirit thus literally gives the mute "utterance" and enables them to assert themselves. . . . By the same principle women who have been specifically marginalized in the Legio leadership, can at least gain a strong voice and a hearing, particularly when they exercise the spiritual gift of prophecy and glossalia.[35]

The Spirit who enables women to participate in the saving work of Jesus, gives women courage, bravery and confidence to raise their voice. From the narration of Caren it can be gleaned how the Spirit enables her to assert herself in front of the male, educated church leaders. She bangs the table three times.

More so, the pneumatology that can be gleaned from Caren's narration addresses issues of who possesses authority to interpret the word of God. Her words "This is the time to be taught by the Holy Spirit" are referring to the illumination by the Holy Spirit which invocation in the mission churches usually is reserved for clergy. Concerning the claim of female authority to interpret the Bible and hence to preach, Musa Dube has argued that women in AICs have developed a particular model of reading the Bible. This is called a "Semoya" reading, that is "of the Spirit."[36] "Moya," the Spirit as God's agent of empowerment and communication with people, offers and justifies the biblical interpretation of "grassroots" women. Dube writes, "[The AICs women] maintain that God's agency is contained in but not limited to the written word. They experience divine communication directly through God's spirit, and they have experienced God's spirit empowering them for human service."[37]

---

33. Joziasse, 201–2.
34. Phiri and Kaunda, "African Instituted Churches," 7.
35. Hinga, "Women, Power and Liberation," 285.
36. Dube, *Postcolonial Feminist Interpretation*, 186–87.
37. Dube, 194.

This interpretative framework implies that women retell and weave their own experiences of healing and empowerment. The pneumatology of AINC women is both biblical and experiential; it is drawn from interpretations of the Scriptures that are contextual and derived from the experiences and the perspectives of women.

The retelling of the salvation history in and through women has indeed destabilizing implications. Hence, another characteristic of the pneumatology as voiced by women in AICs is its potential of bringing about disintegration of systems of domination and subjugation. The narration of Caren can be read as an expression of feminist postcolonial critique. The legitimacy of the exclusive claims of the missionaries of being trained and enabled to interpret the word of God, is questioned. "This is not the time to be taught by human beings" is a powerful protest against the theologically trained clergy and the production of knowledge according to the methods of the Minority World. In AICs pneumatology functions as a critique of hegemonic Christian and cultural power relations.

Conclusion

The faith experiences of women in the AINC express new, previously hidden, perspectives on and aspects of God and divine presence in this world. Women in the AINC attest to the Holy Spirit as a truly life-giving power. In the case of Caren, receiving the life-giving Spirit implies advocating for the healing of relationships and becoming subjects in community. It also means going against unjust power relations, whether sociocultural, ecclesial, raced or gendered, which deny the full humanity of women and men. The immanence of the Triune God, the testimony of the presence of the Holy Spirit in leaders and ordinary members, accounts for an egalitarian community and enables women to take their rightful place in the community of God regardless of gender, race or age. And more so, the pneumatology of women in the AINC attests of life in abundance for the entire community of God.

Bibliography

African Israel Nineveh Church. "Sheria za African Israel Nineveh Church." Nairobi, May 8, 1993.
Anderson, Allan. "African Initiated Churches of the Spirit and Pneumatology." *Word & World* 23, no. 2 (Spring 2003): 178–86.
Clark, Elizabeth A. *Women in the Early Church*. Collegeville: Liturgical Press, 2017.

Clifford, Anne M. *Introducing Feminist Theology*. Maryknoll: Orbis Books, 2001.
Dube, Musa W. *Postcolonial Feminist Interpretation of the Bible*. St. Louis, MO: Chalice Press, 2000.
Hinga, Teresia Mbari. "Women, Power and Liberation in an African Church: A Theological Case Study of the Legio Maria Church in Kenya." PhD diss., University of Lancaster, 1990.
Hoehler-Fatton, Cynthia. *Women of Fire and Spirit: History, Faith, and Gender in Roho Religion in Western Kenya*. New York: Oxford University Press, 1996.
Joziasse, Heleen. "Women's Faith Seeking Life: Lived Christologies and the Transformation of Gender Relations in Two Kenyan Churches." PhD diss., Utrecht University, 2020.
Kgatle, Mookgo Solomon. "A Remarkable Woman in African Independent Churches: Examining Christina Nku's Leadership in St John's Apostolic Faith Mission." *Studia Historiae Ecclesiasticae* 45, no. 1 (2019): 1–14.
Kivuli, Archbishop John M., II. "The Modernization of an African Independent Church." In *Freedom and Interdependence*, edited by Stan Nussbaum, 58–68. Nairobi: Organization of African Instituted Churches, 1994.
Kudoyi, Peter Wilson. "African Israel Nineveh Church: A Theological and Socio-Historical Analysis." Thesis, Kenyatta University, 1991.
Madigan, Kevin, and Carolyn Osiek. *Ordained Women in the Early Church: A Documentary History*. Baltimore, MD: John Hopkins University Press, 2011.
Migliore, Daniel L. *Faith Seeking Understanding: An Introduction to Christian Theology*. Grand Rapids, MI: Eerdmans, 2004.
Mwaura, Philomena. "Gender and Power in African Christianity: African Instituted Churches and Pentecostal Churches." In *African Christianity: An African Story*, edited by Ogbu Kalu, 410–45. Perspectives of Christianity Series 5. Pretoria: University of Pretoria, 2005.
Nadar, Sarojini. "'Stories Are Data with Soul' – Lessons from Black Feminist Epistemology." *Agenda* 28, no. 1 (2014): 18–28.
Phiri, Isabel A., and Chammah J. Kaunda. "African Instituted Churches, Pneumatology and Gender Justice in the Work of GC Oosthuizen: An African Feminist Pneumatological Perspective." *Scriptura* 115 (2016): 1–12.
Sackey, Brigid M. *New Directions in Gender and Religion: The Changing Status of Women in African Independent Churches*. Lanham: Lexington Books, 2006.
Slee, Nicole. "The Holy Spirit and Spirituality." In *The Cambridge Companion to Feminist Theology*, edited by Susan Frank Parsons, 171–89. Cambridge: Cambridge University Press, 2002.
Stephenson, Lisa M. "Where the Wind Blows: Pneumatology in Feminist Perspective." In *T&T Clark Handbook of Pneumatology*, edited by Daniel Castelo and Kenneth M. Loyer, 327–36. London: Bloomsbury, 2020.
Taylor, Joan E., and Ilaria L. E. Ramelli. *Patterns of Women's Leadership in Early Christianity*. Oxford: Oxford University Press, 2021.

Torjesen, Karen J. *When Women Were Priests: Women's Leadership in the Early Church and the Scandal of Their Subordination in the Rise of Christianity*. San Francisco: HarperCollins, 1995.

Welbourn, Frederick B., and Bethwell A. Ogot. *A Place to Feel at Home: A Study of Two Independent Churches in Western Kenya*. London: Oxford University Press, 1966.

7

The Comparative Study of the Work of the Holy Spirit in African Independent Churches and African Pentecostal Churches in Botswana

Kenosi Molato

Researcher, SHINE Africa Project in Gaborone, Botswana

Abstract

The work of the Holy Spirit is crucial in Christianity at large but more so in African Christianity, to such an extent that a church that does not reflect the work of the Holy Spirit, especially the gifts of the Holy Spirit, is considered to be dry, dead and consequently, incompetent in dealing with African problems. Moreover, in Botswana both the Pentecostal churches (APCs) and African Independent Churches (AICs) are known as the churches that demonstrate the work of the Holy Spirit. However, Pentecostal churches demonize the work of the Holy Spirit in AICs arguing that it is not the Holy Spirit who is at work in the AICs but the ancestral spirits. On the other hand, the AICs argue that the same Holy Spirit who is at work in AICs, who manifests himself with signs of healing, possession and speaking in tongues, is the same as the one who works in the Pentecostal churches. Therefore, this paper seeks to compare and contrast the work of the Holy Spirit in the AICs and APCs in Botswana in the light of the work of the Spirit in the biblical text.

Key words: African Pentecostal churches, African Independent Churches, African Traditional Religion, Holy Spirit, Spirit possession, speaking in tongues, spiritual sickness, honor and shame

Introduction

African Pentecostal churches[1] and African Independent Churches are churches that have similar "belonging," namely, that they exist mostly in the African region. There is even some debate that most AICs come from the African Pentecostal churches, although the same could be said of the African Pentecostal churches originating from the AICs. An example can be noted in Southern Africa whereby the Zion Christian Church founder was a member of Apostolic Faith Mission.[2] Furthermore, some scholars such as Monyai argue that the term AICs also incorporates African Pentecostal churches.[3] Monyai goes even further by labeling both the AICs and APCs as African Initiated Churches.[4] Here in Botswana, where the author resides, some of the AICs use Pentecostal names.[5] It is to be denoted that since both the AICs and APCs exist in the African region they both share the same worldview, meaning that the members of these churches are African and have African perspectives of life and experience. However, despite similar origins, there exists a tension between the members of these churches in Botswana.[6] Jacob Born points out that the APCs identify the AICs in Botswana using shaming terms such as *dikereke tsa matemone* (churches of demons), *dikereke tsa bosigo* (night churches), *dikereke tea sephiri* (secret churches) and *dikereke tea metsi* (water churches).[7]

At the center of this shaming and demonization of one another is the work attributed to the Holy Spirit as revealed through prophecy, healing, visions, discerning of the spirits, discerning of witchdoctors and causes of

---

1. This paper chooses to use the term "African" Pentecostal churches in the sense that these are Pentecostal churches that have their origin in Africa. Though they have American influences, they are primarily African churches. Nigerian theologian Ogbu Kalu coined this term in his work *African Pentecostalism: An Introduction* (2008).

2. Hollenwenger, a scholar of African Pentecostalism, attributes the formation of both the AICs and the APCs to the Azuza Street Revival thereby naming the AICs as Pentecostal churches (Hollenwenger, *The Pentecostals*, 151).

3. Monyai, "African Face of Christianity."

4. Monyai.

5. Although not currently a member of an APC church, I was saved in an APC church and studied in an APC Bible College, before going on to seminary.

6. Sundkler, *Bantu Prophets in South Africa*.

7. Born, "'Worlds of the Spirit.'"

illnesses and curing of diseases, the indwelling of the Holy Spirit and speaking in tongues. Songs with lyrics such as "Pour out your spirit Father [*Tshela Moya o o galalelang Ntate*], pour out your spirit so that the earth may be saved [*Tshela moya wa gago go re lefatshe le bolokwe*]" depict a strong yearning and a desire for the Holy Spirit to take control and lead the church.[8] Moreover, both the AICs and APCs in Botswana have an encompassing term that is used to describe the graphic work of the Holy Spirit namely, "the church of the Spirit" (*Dikereke tsa Moya*). Since most of these manifestations are conspicuous in the gathering of both these churches one might argue that these churches are the same, but on the ground there is demonization of each other in relation to the perceived work of the Holy Spirit, using derogatory terms. Consequently, this paper seeks to investigate the work of the Holy Spirit in these churches by doing a comparative analysis of what they term as the evidence of the work of the Holy Spirit, and then provide a biblical view of the work of the Holy Spirit as a form of critical evaluation of the way in which the Holy Spirit is perceived as working in both the AICs and APCs.

Therefore, this paper will (1) explore the current scholarship of the work of the Holy Spirit in the APCs and in the AICs in Botswana, (2) present the context of historical theology in relation to the work of the Holy Spirit, (3) present the biblical motif of the work of the Holy Spirit, (4) highlight a comparative analysis of the work of the Holy Spirit of the AICs and the PCS and (5) bring a concluding analysis.

The Current Scholarship of the Work of the Holy Spirit in APCs and in the AICs in Botswana

In his study of both the AICs and APCs in Botswana, Born argues that the Holy Spirit is perceived as the "all-embracing, pervading power of God."[9] Consequently there is a slight change of emphasis from the classical view of the Holy Spirit, learned from the Western missionaries and mainline churches, which leans more toward the Spirit enabling a lifestyle of holiness.[10]

Furthermore, Born has observed that one of the main quests for the Holy Spirit in the AICs, especially in the church he studied (Hermon Church), is based on those who seek spiritual experiences.[11] Born goes further to note that

---

8. Molato, "Comparative Study of Prophesy."
9. Born, "'Worlds of the Spirit,'" 121.
10. Born, 121.
11. Born, 121.

this quest for spiritual experience is indicated by the songs they sing: "Pour out the Spirit, Father" (*Tshela Moya, Ntate*); "We give thanks for the connection with the glorious Spirit" (*Re lebogela kopano ya Moya o o galalelang*); "We cry for the Spirit" (*Re lelela Moya*); "Pour out your glorious Spirit so that the earth may be saved" (*Tsholela Moya o o galalelang, lefatshe le bolokwe*). The main reason for seeking spiritual experiences is to be possessed by the Spirit (*go tshwarwa ke Moya*), and when one has arrived at this state they lose control of themselves. Born states that though this state is being longed for in the AICs, it is also being feared because one tends to lose control of their actions.[12]

Another experience, which Born had observed at Hermon Church in Botswana, is what is called "spiritual sickness" (*Bolwetse jwa semoya*). He notes that this condition is believed to show that God has called you. This sickness does not leave the individual until they respond to God's call in their life.[13] Moreover, I came across this concept when I studied the Botswana Healing Church. In this church (Botswana Healing Church) spiritual sickness acts as a way of receiving prophetic visions from God.[14]

In Hermon Church (HC) gatherings, they speak of sensing the presence of the Holy Spirit in their bodies. They point out that they feel a small breeze moving in their bodies or they hear a voice speaking to them.[15] Born captures the scenario in which they sense the presence of God had come upon their gathering, "but suffice it for now to note that the sight of church members jerking in unusual ways, falling to the ground, staggering, crying, laughing, whistling, sighing loudly, burping or speaking in 'tongues' (unknown 'spiritual' languages) has a powerful effect on all who are present."[16]

Born, in his analysis of an APC's church named Good News Ministries (GM), notes that in this church the Holy Sprit is related with impersonal manners with phrases such as the "fire of God" and the "power of God."[17] According to GM, the Holy Spirit is depicted as fire both in the Old and New Testament.[18] In a sermon that the pastor of GM preached, focusing on Acts 1:8, he spoke eloquently noting that God has called the church to be powerful and that the church needs to move in power. He alluded to the idea that when

---

12. Born, 121.
13. Born, 121.
14. Molato, "Comparative Study of," 56.
15. Born, "'Worlds of the Spirit,'" 99.
16. Born, 99.
17. Born, 125.
18. Born, 125.

the Holy Spirit comes upon the church it is transformed to be a powerful church.[19] The Holy Spirit in GM is perceived as an explosive force that is able to annihilate the believer's problem.[20]

In his analysis of the work of the Holy Spirit in Good News Ministries, Born argues that in this church,

> The baptism of the Holy Spirit and fire is a one-time, second work of God which enables GM members to speak with other tongues, and fills them with power so that they can emerge victorious in their spiritual lives. The filling of the Holy Spirit and fire is available continuously and is experienced as a daily renewal of spiritual power for holy living.[21]

Moreover, though this church focuses on the impersonal power of the Holy Spirit there are elements of the personal aspects that are being emphasized, such as that the Holy Spirit is a helper who teaches the believers and also that he helps the believers in their prayer lives.[22]

The similarity that emerges from Born's study of both Hermon Church (an AIC) and Good News Ministries (an APC) is that both churches focus on the power of the Holy Spirit. They both desire to meet the needs of their communities, who perceive life from an African worldview in which life is a battlefield because of a competition for honor through superior power. Differences also emerge in that the Hermon Church (AIC) relates with the Holy Spirit more in a personal manner such as the comforter and the healer, while the Good News Ministries (APC) relate with the Holy Spirit in an impersonal manner such as the fire of God and the power of God.[23] Born holds that "While HC usually describes the Spirit as 'shining/glorious' (*o o galalelang*), GM prefers the English usage of 'Holy.' It is possible that the HC descriptor may focus on the revelatory or prophetic nature of the Spirit, whereas the GM adjective emphasizes the moral."[24]

In the study done by Monyai between 1982 and 1988 on the African Initiated Churches[25] he asked his respondents the question,

---

19. Born, 125.
20. Born, 125.
21. Born, 126.
22. Born, 126.
23. Born, 127.
24. Born, 127.
25. Monyai uses African Initiated Churches to refer to both the AICs and the APCs churches.

Who is the Holy Spirit? The following answers were given: He is Jesus Christ, he is the Spirit of God, he is an angel of the Lord, he is the Spirit associated with good deeds, he is faith and he is the one who helps Christians foresee oncoming events, the Holy Spirit is also perceived as a member of the Trinity because he is called God and the everlasting Spirit.[26]

These answers suggest that there is a confusion regarding the concept of the Trinity, the deity of the Holy Spirit and the person of the Holy Spirit. The answers given by Monyai's participants differ from the study done by Obed Kealotswe on Head Mountain Church (AIC) whereby he argued that the Head Mountain Church members do understand the concept of the Trinity and the deity of the Holy Spirit, and that this church had not moved away from the teaching that they have received from the mainline churches and the missionaries.[27] Furthermore, in the church that Monyai studied, the Trinity is perceived in a hierarchical structure with the Holy Spirit viewed as third in this hierarchy.[28] These churches express the relationship between the Holy Spirit and the other members of the Trinity in that the Holy Spirit is found in both God the Father and the God the Son.[29] These churches further articulate the relationship between the Holy Spirit and other members of the Trinity by stating that with regard to the redemptive plan, God the Father is the one who controls the Holy Spirit, thereby he sent Jesus Christ by the Holy Spirit. Consequently, the Holy Spirit is a representative and a messenger of both God the Father and the Son.[30]

With reference to the work of the Holy Spirit, the churches that were studied by Monyai indicate the Holy Spirit is the power of God and admonishes people to live lives that reflect Christ.[31] It should be noted that this conclusion slightly differs with Born who argued that there is no emphasis on moral behavior in the AICs, which he studied.[32] Furthermore, the participants interviewed by Monyai pointed out that when a believer has done something wrong they need to confess their wrongdoing to the Holy Spirit.[33] It is believed

---

26. Monyai, "African Face of Christianity," 171.
27. Kealotswe, "Doctrine and Rituals," 247.
28. Monyai, "African Face of Christianity," 172.
29. Monyai, 173.
30. Monyai, 173.
31. Monyai, 173.
32. Born, "'Worlds of the Spirit.'"
33. Monyai, "African Face of Christianity," 173.

that the Holy Spirit heals those who confess their sins and repent from their wrongdoing.[34]

Kealotswe in his study of Head Mountain Church (AIC) in Botswana investigated the doctrines of this church. With regard to the Holy Spirit, the emphasis is mostly that the Holy Spirit is the comforter.[35] He argues that this emphasis of the Holy Spirit should be understood in relation to the view of death that this church subscribes to.[36] In Head Mountain Church, it is believed that when death occurs people must mourn for the one who has departed, since to lose the loved one is something that affects the believers. The believers should pray for the promise Jesus gave his disciples that the comforter might come to comfort them.[37] This is based on the Head Mountain Church minister, who is from the Kalanga culture, which does not accept death. Therefore, the Holy Spirit as the comforter is contextualized in order to address the needs of the society.

Historical Theology of the Work of the Holy Spirit in AICs and APCs

Church historian Carl Trueman once noted that every legitimate question requires a legitimate answer.[38] Consequently, what led to the formation of AICs and APCs was the question, How can the Holy Spirit deal with the African issues? The formation of APCs and AICs was based on a longing of the move of the Spirit to address African issues for the mainline churches, which were mostly planted by western missionaries that failed to address this question.[39] E. A. Asamoah captures this when he postulates,

> it is exaggeration to say that the church attitude towards African belief has generally been one of negations, a denial of the validity of these spirits. Anybody who knows the African Christianity intimately will know that no amount of denial on the part of the

---

34. Monyai, 173.
35. Kealotswe, "Doctrine and," 247.
36. Kealotswe, 247.
37. Kealotswe, 247.
38. Trueman, "Lecture 01: The Reformation."
39. Adodeji Adewuya notes that though lack of expressive worship and the work of the Holy Spirit has led to both AICs and the APCs to break out of the mainline churches the expressive worship can be seen in the mainline churches today in Africa and this is due to the influence of APCs and the AICs on the mainline churches.

church will expel belief in supernatural powers from the minds of the African people.[40]

Consequently, the failure of the mainline churches to address the spirituality of African people prompted many African people to leave mainline churches and form their own. South African theologian Tinyiko Maluleke terms this desire as the "longing to be engaged with the grass roots of public theology."[41] The formation of the Pentecostal movement in Azusa Street in 1903 was in a black African-American church and was depicted by the emphases of baptism of the Holy Spirit, speaking in tongues and miraculous gifts. Therefore, evidence of the grass roots theology was conspicuous in these gatherings. Scholars such as MacRobert argue that this formation of the Pentecostal movement in a Black American church with the strong desire of the move of the Holy Spirit, can be traced in Black slavery and thus reflects the African religious experience of spirituality.[42] Nile Harper's book titled *Urban Churches: Vital Signs* captures the essence of the history of the Black church in America with its emphasis of worship: "Black churches have always borne centrality to corporate worship that offers strong therapy to aid the congregation in coping with everyday situations, offering hope that someday things will change."[43] Leonard Lovett argues that "It may be categorically stated that black Pentecostalism emerged out of the context of the brokenness of black existence . . . their holistic view of religion had its roots in African religion."[44]

Researchers such as MacRobert have highlighted comparative analysis between African religion and the work of the Holy Spirit in African churches.[45] In his work, MacRobert quotes Herskovits who suggests that the common evidence of the Holy Spirit possession, which is seen among both the AICs and APCs, is not a Eurocentric concept, but rather reflects African indigenous religions.[46] MacRobert continues to note that "rhythmic hand clapping, the antiphonal participation of the congregation in the sermon, the immediacy of God in the services and baptism by immersion, are all survivals of Africanisms."[47] However, Allan Anderson, a predominant researcher of Pentecostalism in

---

40. Asamoa, "Christian Church and African Heritage," 297.
41. Maluleke, "Theological Interest in AICs," 19.
42. MacRobert, *Black Roots and White Racism*, 77–78.
43. Harper, *Urban Churches: Vital signs*.
44. Leonard Lovett (1999: 9).
45. MacRobert, *Black Roots and White Racism*.
46. MacRobert, 29.
47. MacRobert, 29.

Africa, questions this conclusion suggesting that we should not be quick to point to these manifestations, which have a biblical support, as just African religion, but rather this must be seen as remolding Christianity to fit in African space.[48] Whether it is remolding grassroots theology or adaptive transformative theory, at the center of the formation of both the APCs and the AICs was a desire to reflect and engage African worldview and cosmology. This calls for caution so that the danger of diluting the biblical truths is avoided.

Consequently, this raises the question of the historicity of the origins of both the APCs and the AICs. Historically, the work of the Holy Spirit with the evidence of miraculous power is attributed to have begun in Azusa Street in America. However, there is also strong evidence to suggest that the miraculous work of the Holy Spirit is also indigenous in the African continent.[49] A proponent of this view is African Pentecostal scholar Ogbu Kalu. He argues that African Pentecostalism emerges from the missionary church thereby appropriating the missionary gospel message to be able to adapt to the African context.[50] Scenarios have been provided such as of Shembe who broke out of a Baptist church in 1911 and started prophesying and speaking in tongues without any influence from Azusa Street influences. Another example is of Sebolao who broke out of London Missionary Society in Botswana in 1935 and started performing miraculous powers and prophesied. Stories have been told of his followers who were persecuted by the government and put in prisons.[51] Moreover, practices such as spirit possession are common in African Traditional Religion (ATR), which raises the question of whether there is a direct correlation between this phenomenon in ATR and African Christianity as it is depicted in both the AICs and APCs. Grace Harris in a study she had done among the Kenyan tribes demonstrated the existence of spirit possession in these tribes. She noted that a person possessed by the Spirit often speaks in foreign languages.[52] Just like in AICs and APCs, the person who is spirit possessed makes themself to be receptive of revelatory words from the ancestors.[53]

---

48. Anderson, *Moya*, 27.
49. Liardon, *God's Generals*.
50. Kalu, *African Pentecostalism*, 8.
51. Kealotswe, "Doctrine and Rituals," 66.
52. Harris, "Possession 'Hysteria,'" 1046.
53. Harris, 1046.

Perspective of the Holy Spirit in the AICs in Botswana

So in consideration of the scholarship and historical context, it becomes evident that the Holy Spirit's place in the AICs in Botswana is prominent. Their theology deems the Holy Spirit as the Spirit of God, he is Jesus and he is understood as the angel of God.[54] There is an affirmation on the AICs that the Holy Spirit is a member of the Trinity, but how does the Holy Spirit relate to other members of the Trinity? The AICs postulate that the Holy Spirit is an active member of the Trinity, in that when God wanted to save humankind he sent the Holy Spirit into the womb of Mary, and thus resulted in Jesus being born. In this way the Holy Spirit is Jesus, hence Jesus was born out of the Holy Spirit.

The Holy Spirit is seen "as the all-embracing, pervading power of God."[55] This makes one tend to believe that the work of the Spirit takes a central role in this church compared to the other members of the Trinity, since the emphasis in their gathering is on the works of the Spirit of God, as revealed in their healing clinics and prophecy. Monyai argues that the AICs have poor Christology hence the overemphasis on the work of the Spirit.[56] Moreover, the emphasis in their gathering is not holiness, which the Holy Spirit causes the believers to long for, but rather the power of God. This is due to the fact that the church wants to respond to the crisis of their society, which is predominantly pervaded by the spiritual realities. Therefore, they feel that if they don't demonstrate the power of God in their churches then their members will not trust Christ but will go back to African Traditional Religions.[57]

The Holy Spirit is perceived as the angel of the Lord in the AICs.[58] In Maun Healing Church this angel is said to be green in color. This angel, who is said to be Holy Spirit, plays a major role in healing clinics. He is believed to guide the prophets and those that are involved in leading the church. It is said that when this angel appears in a church gathering the presence of God fills the building to such an extent that no one can be able to stand on their feet in the church. It is believed that when this angel appears it is because he has a word from God that he wants to give to the worshippers.[59]

---

54. Monyai, "African Face of Christianity," 175.
55. Anderson, "Pentecostal Pneumatology," 73 in Born, "Worlds of the Spirit," 24.
56. Monyai, 175.
57. Kealotswe, "Doctrine and Rituals," 66.
58. Monyai, "African Face of Christianity."
59. Molato, "Comparative Study of Prophesy."

The primary work of the Holy Spirit in these churches is to possess the believers. Monyai notes that this possession occurs for both sexes.[60] The Spirit possesses women because they are weak and he also possesses men because they are leaders of the family, therefore, they need power to properly lead their household.[61] Those that are possessed with the Holy Spirit are believed to be the modern-day prophets for they have a message from God. Therefore, the possession of the Spirit entails that an individual who is possessed functions in the same way the prophets of the Old Testament functioned. Monyai argues that one who is possessed with the Holy Spirit, (1) is to be prayed for, (2) needs to be calmed down, (3) needs to be pleased, and (4) needs to be listened at this moment since it is believed that they have a special word of God.[62] In dealing with how are they possessed by the Holy Spirit the participants noted the following: (1) the angel enters them, (2) too much Spirit enters them during baptism, and (3) they have too much faith, which guarantees that the Spirit will come upon them.

The reasons they contend why believers are possessed by the Holy Spirit is that, (1) they can chase sin away from the believers and the church; (2) in the state of possession, the prophets are informed about the mission they are to undertake; (3) it is because one has been shown a revelation that they need to prophesy about; and (4) it is because one has entered a particular state of mind to make themselves more receptive to the Lord.[63]

Perspective of the Work of the Holy Spirit in APCs in Botswana

The APCs in Botswana hold that a true believer must be baptized with the Holy Spirit, with evidence of speaking in tongues and this sets the believers as separated from the world because they are born again and have been transformed by the power of God. This baptism is central to understanding the theology of APCs. They argue that someone can be saved without being baptized with the Holy Spirit. But if you are not baptized by the Holy Spirit, you will not be effective for the service of Christ. They point to the passage in Acts 1:8 whereby the disciples were informed by Christ to wait for the power

---

60. Molato, 173.
61. Monyai, "African Face of Christianity," 173.
62. Monyai, 173.
63. Monyai, 176.

of the Holy Spirit to come upon them and then they will be effective witnesses of Christ.[64]

Moreover, to demonstrate that someone is born again APCs believe they need to speak in tongues. Wessels notes, "It serves as a 'bridge-burning' act. After that there is no turning back. It is also a rite of passage, introducing the person to a new existence, and assuring that she has indeed been initiated into the new state of existence and empowered to act accordingly."[65] Furthermore, the act of speaking in tongues is used to activate the power of God and makes the believer connected to God. APCs also hold on to the view that when you speak in tongues you trick the enemy for you speak mysteries. Consequently, the believers are encouraged to speak in tongues in their prayer meetings.

The term "born again" is highly used in Botswana to refer to the APCs. This is due to the emphasis of this concept in their power evangelism crusades. Born notes,

> GM members argue that they can confidently challenge people to live a transformed life because the Spirit of God empowers them to live the way God intended. They boldly approach new people on the street, at work, while riding public transit and in their neighborhoods and share the Good News message. They seem to have little or no fear; and the reason for this assurance is that they are born again Christians who have been baptized in the Spirit.[66]

Moreover, the concept of viewing the Holy Spirit as the fire is very popular in the APCs in Botswana to such an extent that they are often called "fire churches." This is because in their gatherings the worshippers will often shout the word "fire" in order to try to annihilate some spiritual problems. They argue that the God whom they serve is a God of fire therefore when they shout "fire" they are calling the fire of the Holy Spirit to consume their problem.

Biblical Motif of the Work of the Holy Spirit

In this section, this paper presents the biblical motifs of the Holy Spirit. It will examine the Scripture passages that present the deity, person and the work of the Holy Spirit. Furthermore, it will look at the key passages that are used

---

64. Born, "'Worlds of the Spirit.'"
65. Wessels, "Charismatic Christian Congregations," 360–74.
66. Born, "'Worlds of the Spirit,'" 1080.

to form the foundations of both the APCs and AICs. This is based on the fact that these churches claim that what they do is based on the Bible.

The Person of the Holy Spirit

The Bible repeatedly speaks of the Holy Spirit, known also as the Spirit of God (Gen 1:2) and the Spirit of Jesus Christ. It indicates that the Holy Spirit is of the same essence as the Father and the Son. Hence the Nicene Creed was formulated after interrogating the biblical doctrine of "Trinity," thereby establishing what is commonly the orthodox view of the Triune God. Therefore, to establish the biblical warrant for the deity of the Holy Spirit one has to look for passages that equate the attributes of God the Father and the Son with the Holy Spirit. In John 14:16 Jesus promised his disciples the following, "And I will ask the Father, and he will give you another Helper, to be with you forever" (ESV). Since Jesus was about to leave this world, he promised his disciples that he would send the comforter, who is the Holy Spirit. But note the attribute that Jesus gives to the Holy Spirit. He, the Holy Spirit, will be with the disciples forever or for eternity. This entails that just as God the Father and the Son are eternal, the Holy Spirit is also eternal. Moreover also this implies that the Holy Spirit coexists with both God the Father and the Son. Another characteristic attributed to the Holy Spirit in the Scripture is holiness. Holiness is a characteristic of the Holy Spirit since the adjective "Holy" is used to modify "Spirit." Therefore since the Holy Spirit is holy in essence, he can be blasphemed. Jesus taught about the holiness of the Holy Spirit noting that whosoever blasphemes the Holy Spirit will not be forgiven (Matt 12:32).

The Works of the Holy Spirit

The Holy Spirit in the Old and New Testament empowered people to serve God. This demonstrated the inadequacy of men's strength to function in God's service. In the OT we see God empowering Joshua to take over the huge task of leading the children of Israel after the death of Moses (Num 27:18; Deut 34:9). God, in this narrative of Joshua, gives him wisdom and leadership skills, which Joshua needed to carry forth this task (Num 27:18). These scenarios of being empowered for service are conspicuously seen in the life of Samson and the lives of the Judges (Judg 3:18; 13:25), and in David as he served as king and was fearful that his sin would mean the Holy Spirit being removed from him. Finally, and most importantly in the Old Testament is when it is predicted that the Holy Spirit would anoint the Messiah with power (Isa 11:2–3).

It is often believed that the Holy Spirit enters, leaves and re-enters a person depending on their obedience or disobedience. However, this focuses on the OT (such as the example of Saul in 1 Samuel 16 and 19), rather than the promises of the Holy Spirit's presence given in the NT. As we progress into the NT the Holy Spirit, rather than coming "upon" people to empower for a particular task comes to indwell/seal us as God's possession (belonging to him forever) to fill us, live in and through us.

One of the works of the Holy Spirit in the Bible is to sanctify, that is to cleanse the believers from sin. It is the primary duty of God the Father to transform us to the image of his dear Son, and the member of the Trinity who is responsible to perform this duty is the person of the Holy Spirit (1 Cor 6:11). Moreover, in the lives of the believers the Holy Spirit acts as the purifying agent, restraining them from sin by convicting them (John 16:8–11).

Gifts of the Spirit

The gifts of the Holy Spirit are central in the life of the local church because the gifts that the Holy Spirit gives to the believers enables them to serve one another and reach out to the world (1 Cor 12:1). It is to be noted that the gifts the Holy Spirit gives are not for individual use and for self-promotion but they are given so that the believers should serve one another (1 Cor 14). While they are important and vital for the ministry of the church and for the building up of the church, all must be done with the "more excellent" way of love in mind (1 Cor 12 and 13) – love is the first of the fruit of the spirit. We often assume that the evidence of the power of God in the gifts is by obvious signs and wonders such as a healing service, but there can be a neglect of the fact that the true evidence of the power of God is to be demonstrated in how much the gifts operate by the way of love (1 Cor 13:1–3).

Fruit of the Spirit

The Holy Spirit not only works outside of believers in terms of serving others, he first works from within by transforming them into the character of Christ (Rom 8:29), which results in the good works. Thus, he brings forth the fruit of the Spirit in believers – love, joy, peace, patience, kindness, goodness, gentleness, faithfulness and self-control (Gal 5:22–23). These qualities, which the Holy Spirit works in the believers, reflect the character of God. Consequently, the believers are required to live according to this fruit in everything they do in this world. The more believers desire to exhibit the fruit of the Spirit the more they will be effective in their service for God (2 Pet 1:8–9).

Comparative Analysis

This section compares and contrasts main concepts that are common in both the AICs and the APCs, with regard to the works of the Holy Spirit using the biblical criteria to investigate the weakness and the strength of each view. This paper chooses to use biblical criteria based on the fact that churches in Africa acknowledge their desire to adhere to the Bible as their source of authority.[67]

The first major confusion in the AICs in Botswana is on the issue of who is the person of the Holy Spirit. The answer to this question leads to many conclusions, such as he is the angel of God. The Bible clearly attributes the Holy Spirit with deity. He is fully God and not just a manifestation or form of God as an angel who comes like Gabriel who visited Mary. On the other hand, the APCs generally view the Holy Spirit as a member of the Trinity and not just an angel. However, some APCs believe that the Holy Spirit is a form or mode of how God manifests himself rather than him being a full person of the Trinity. This leads to the heretical view called modalism, which was refuted by early church councils.[68] Consequently, the similarity of the concept of modalism resurfaces here but the difference is how it is expressed. In the AICs it is expressed through an angel while in APCs it is expressed by the manifestations of the Spirit.

A second major confusion is in relation to Spirit possession in the AICs and the infilling of the Holy Spirit in the APCs. Though the AICs use the term "possession" and the APCs uses "infilling," the concept is the same, as it is portrayed by falling on the floor, speaking in tongues and receiving revelatory messages.[69] Though both churches point to a biblical text as a warrant for their practice, the Bible does not allow believers to lose control in such a way that there's disorder and chaos in the gathering of the believers. In 1 Corinthians 14, the apostle Paul exhorts believers to do things in an orderly way. Therefore, a mark of proper spirit possession and infilling of the Holy Spirit is depicted by orderliness in the church gathering. Neither is spirit possession in Scripture a mark of superiority or demonstrated by having superior gifts such as prophecy,

---

67. Mbiti, *African Religions and Philosophy*, 74.
68. Modalism was rejected by churches from the late fifth or early sixth century in favor of a Trinitarian view such as later outlined in the Athanasian Creed.
69. Born, "'Worlds of the Spirit,'" 121.

but the Holy Spirit's indwelling is the privilege of all Christians who are called to fulfill their equally valuable roles/giftings in the body of Christ (1 Cor 12).

The third major issue is confusion over the purpose of the power of the Holy Spirit that leads to a lack of emphasis on the Holy part of the Spirit in the AICs although it is the major strength in the APCs in Botswana. The APCs argue that a believer is born again and transformed by the power of the Holy Spirit and the life of a believer must reflect Christ who is holy. But on the AICs side the emphasis is more on the external power, which can bring healing to the believers.[70] Therefore, it will be wise for the AICs to acknowledge that it is not un-biblical for the APCs to pursue holiness. The Holy Spirit purifies the believers and makes them yearn for holiness. Both can fall prey to the possibility of wrongly seeing power for greater holiness than others, or particular power to perform healings, as means of elevating a person "above" others in a subtle desire for honor/status.

A fourth issue is the emphasis of speaking in tongues to show that a believer is baptized with the Holy Spirit in the APCs. Though this concept can be seen in the AICs, it is not common. Therefore, speaking in tongues is practiced in both the AICs and APCs but it used differently to achieve different results. In the APCs it is used to access the supernatural realm and is used as a language that is believed to trick Satan. In the AICs the goal of speaking in tongues is not clear, but what is clear is that when one speaks in tongues, they have reached a highest degree of spirituality. While the concept of speaking in tongues is in the bible, there is no scriptural warrant that demands that every believer should speak in tongues. The apostle Paul in 1 Corinthians 12 demonstrates that speaking in tongues is a gift and this entails that some might have it and others may not have it.[71] And those that have it are not of greater spiritual significance or status than others. Furthermore, the apostle Paul argues that this gift should be used to edify the body not for self-focused use (1 Cor 14).

Both APCs and AICs define themselves as the church of the Spirit with the emphasis on the Holy Spirit over the other members of the Trinity, thereby leading to poor Christology and a poor view of God the Father. This on its own is a major concern. The role of the Holy Spirit is not to take the limelight, that is why the scripture describes the Holy Spirit as the Spirit of God and the Spirit of Christ. Jesus taught that when the Holy Spirit came he would

---

70. Born, 121.

71. This paper chooses not to debate whether the gift of tongues was just an apostolic gift that ceased to operate post apostolic era.

glorify Christ rather than glorifying himself.⁷² On the grassroots level, these churches might be receiving honor or status by branding themselves as the Spirit centered churches but from a biblical point of view this is not an honor state but a reproach to the one whom they are trying to please if their honor is being sought other than from God alone as revealed in the Scriptures.

Concluding Analysis

This paper sought to compare and to contrast the work of the Holy Spirit in APCs and AICs in Botswana. To achieve this goal the paper presented the recent scholarship of the work of the Holy Spirit in both the AICs and APCs in Botswana. It demonstrated the new perspectives, which have emerged from various scholars who investigated different churches throughout Botswana. This paper chose to have a holistic approach that represents both the APCs and the AICs throughout the country. In the second section, the paper outlined the historicity of the APCs and the AICs and investigated if this phenomenon has been imposed into Africa or if it is indigenous to Africa hence the name "African" Pentecostalism and "African" Independent Churches. It demonstrated that this phenomenon is indigenous in the sense that spirituality is embedded within the African worldview and that the honorable degree of spirituality is what each and every African worshipper seeks to attain whether in ATR or in African Christianity.

In the third section, the paper presented the perspective of the work of the Holy Spirit in the AICs and the APCs highlighting the key concepts on both sides. These key concepts such as speaking in tongues, spiritual possession and spiritual sickness emerged from reviewing the literature depicting the commonality of the concepts from both sides. Consequently, indicating that the shaming of the AICs by the APCs cannot be justified. The fourth section presented the biblical motif of the work of the Holy Spirit. This is based on the fact that both churches claim their allegiance to the Bible as the word of God and that Scripture can support their practices. As such, the biblical motif of the person of the Holy Spirit was outlined with the purpose of viewing both the AICs and APCs doctrine of the person of the Holy Spirit through a biblical foundation. Moreover, the biblical motif of the fruit of the Spirit was presented with the view of pointing out that though both the AICs and APCs tend to find honor in the demonstration of the power of the Spirit, there is greater honor in grounding the practices in Scripture, by manifesting the character of God.

---

72. Grudem, *Systematic Theology*, 634–50.

The final section compared and contrasted the views of the works of the Spirit arising from both churches. The weaknesses and the strengths of each church view were raised with the aim of bringing a dialectic synthesis in the light of the biblical motif. Some key findings emerge in this paper that both of these churches are influenced by the honor/shame worldviews, which permeate their practices such as seeking honor through demonstrations of higher degrees of spirituality, which sets an individual to be perceived as an elite member in the church gathering. In the AICs, spirit possession is perceived as a high degree of spirituality that one can reach. However, this attainment is also feared in the sense that one cannot know what might happen to them when they are high in spiritual degree. In the APCs the spirituality can be attained through the means of being filled with the Spirit. Moreover, few attain this level though every believer is encouraged to seek for this experience. Both AICs and APCs create a "class" category of attaining this high level of spirituality.

More study is certainly warranted on how honor/shame dynamics influence belief and practice in relation to the Holy Spirit in African churches, so that churches can better truly honor God as they allow the Holy Spirit to gift their members and produce his fruit in them for the good of the church and their witness to the world.

Bibliography

Adewuya, J. Ayodeji. "The Effects of the Prosperity Gospel in Africa." In *Spirit Empowered Christianity in the 21st Century: Insights, Analysis, and Future Trends from World-Renowned Scholars*, edited by Vinson Synan, 401–15. Lake Mary: Charisma, 2011.

Anderson, Allan H. "Pentecostal pneumatology and African power concepts continuity or change?" *Missionalia: Southern African Journal of Mission Studies* 19, no. 1 (1991): 65–74.

———. *Moya: The Holy Spirit in African Context*. Pretoria: University of South Africa, 1991.

Asamoa, E. A. "The Christian Church and African Heritage." *International Review of Mission* 44, no. 175 (1955): 292–301.

Born, Jacob Bryan. "'Worlds of the Spirit': Exploring African Spiritual and New Pentecostal Relations in Botswana." DTh diss., Pretoria, University of South Africa, 2009.

Grudem, Wayne. *Systematic Theology: An Introduction to Biblical Doctrine*. Leicester: Inter-Varsity Press, 1994.

Harper, Nile. *Urban Churches: Vital Signs: Beyond Charity toward Justice*. Eugene, OR: Wipf & Stock, 1999.

Harris, Grace. "Possession 'Hysteria' in a Kenya Tribe." *American Anthropologist* 59, no. 6 (December 1957): 1046–66.
Hollenwenger, Walter. *The Pentecostals*. London: SCM, 1972.
Kalu, Ogbu. *African Pentecostalism: An Introduction*. Oxford: Oxford University Press, 2008.
Kealotswe, Obed Ndeya Obadiah. "Doctrine and Rituals in an African Independent Church in Botswana: A Study of the Beliefs, Rituals and Practices of Head Mountain of God Apostolic Church in Zion." PhD diss., Edinburgh, University of Edinburgh, 1993.
Liardon, Roberts. *God's Generals: Why They Succeeded and Why Some Failed*. New Kensington: Whitaker, 2000.
Lovett, Leonardo. *Black Origins of the Pentecostal Movement in Synan, V, Aspects of Pentecostal-Charismatic Origins* (ed). Plainfield: Logos, 1975.
MacRobert, Iain. *The Black Roots and White Racism of Early Pentecostalism in the USA*. New York: Palgrave Macmillan, 1988.
Maluleke, T. M. "Theological Interest in AICs and other Grass-Root Communities." *Journal of Black Theology in South Africa* 10, no. 1 (1996): 41–43.
Mbiti, John S. *African Religions and Philosophy*. 2nd ed. Oxford: Heineman, 1990.
Molato, Kenosi. "Comparative Study of Prophesy between African Independent Churches and African Pentecostal Church in Botswana." Master's thesis, Gaborone, University of Botswana, 2017.
Monyai, Keikanetswe. "An African Face of Christianity: A Theology of Five African Initiated Churches." PhD diss., Potchefstroom, South Africa, North West University, 2007.
Müller, Retief. "The Zion Christian Church and Global Christianity: Negotiating a Tight Rope between Localisation and Globalization." *Religion* 45, no. 2 (2015): 174–90.
Premark, Laura. "Prophets, Evangelists and Missionaries: Trans-Atlantic Interactions in the Emergence of Nigerian Pentecostalism." *Religion* 45, no. 2 (2015): 221–38.
Sundkler, Bengt. *Bantu Prophets in South Africa*. London: Oxford University Press, 1961.
Trueman, Carl. "Lecture 01: The Reformation – Dr. Carl Trueman." The Master's Seminary. Posted 18 January 2017. YouTube video, https://www.youtube.com/watch?v=VEpQjtufzp0&list=PL80a7MMbHQC57islGFgFDXHB76a0Z0VQS.
Wessels, G. Francois. "Charismatic Christian Congregations and Social Justice: A South African Perspective." *Missionalia* 25, no. 3 (1997): 360–74.

8

Perceptions of the Holy Spirit's Deliverance in Ghanaian Charismatic Ministries

Assessing the Work of J. Kwabena Asamoah-Gyadu

Stephanie A. Lowery

Lecturer, Africa International University and Kalamba School of Leadership

and

Danson Ottawa Wafula

Pastoral Intern, Hope City Bible Church, Nairobi, Kenya

Abstract

Examining the works of J. Kwabena Asamoah-Gyadu, this paper explores the view of Ghanaian charismatic ministries (CMs) on the Holy Spirit's role in deliverance, which is seen as a major aspect of sanctification. The paper argues that the CMs have identified some weaknesses in non-CM pneumatology, particularly with regard to the expectation of the Spirit's presence and manifestation in a Christian as well as the necessity and urgency of the Christian's active pursuit of sanctification.

Key words: J. Kwabena Asamoah-Gyadu, deliverance, charismatic ministries, practical salvation, salvation, sanctification, Pentecostal, charismatic

Introduction

It is commonly acknowledged that charismatic movements have swept across the African continent like an unstoppable wildfire. As the fire continues to rage, it behooves the church to ask herself what she can learn from this movement, which has had a profound effect on Christianity as a whole.

Before proceeding, a word on terminology is appropriate. The charismatic or Pentecostal "wave" or "fire" has been described using various terms. Some refer to this movement as "Pentecostal and Charismatic," while others prefer one or the other of those terms.[1] For the sake of simplicity and consistency, here we use the term "charismatic ministries," as it is the phrase used by J. Kwabena Asamoah-Gyadu, a Ghanaian scholar who specializes in studying Ghanaian charismatic ministries and whose work is the focus of this paper.

We have chosen Asamoah-Gyadu's works as the primary sources for this paper as he has for some time chronicled and assessed the movement in his own country. In his writings, the phrase "charismatic ministries" (hereafter CMs) refers to "the new wave of independent Pentecostal movements."[2] Asamoah-Gyadu emphasizes that these CMs have roots in orthodoxy, but rather than remain as renewal movements within a mainstream church denomination, they have broken off to form new ministries.[3] Therefore they can be categorized as AICs, African Indigenous Churches.[4]

Asamoah-Gyadu possesses an emic (or insider's) perspective on Pentecostal/charismatic Christianity, and has for years studied CMs within his country and written extensively about them, both with sympathy for their strengths as well as critiques of their shortcomings.[5] He notes that these ministries emphasize "the *experience* of the power of the Holy Spirit and the

---

1. For instance, Allan H. Anderson sometimes refers to the movement as "Pentecostal," while at other times he uses the phrase "Pentecostal and Charismatic" (See Anderson, "Contextualization in Pentecostalism," 34); meanwhile, with reference to Ghana specifically, George Anderson Jr. refers to such ministries as Neo-Prophetic Pentecostal/charismatic (See Anderson, "Ghana's Neo-Prophetic Pentecostal," 16–27).

2. Asamoah-Gyadu, *African Charismatics*, 1.

3. Asamoah-Gyadu, 1, 3.

4. AIC can stand for African Indigenous Churches or African Initiated Churches or African Independent Churches.

5. For instance, see Asamoah-Gyadu, "'Broken Calabashes and Covenants,'" 443.

use of this power to conquer evil."⁶ The Holy Spirit is viewed as a powerful means of combating evil: "The deployment of divine resources, that is power and authority in the name and blood of Jesus – perceived in pneumatological terms as the intervention of the Holy Spirit," provides relief from evil forces.⁷ Allan H. Anderson reinforces this inseparable link between the Spirit and salvation in African Pentecostal movements, characterizing their soteriology as a "pneumatological soteriology."⁸ Anderson's phrase highlights that in these movements, strong emphasis is placed on the Spirit's ongoing role in a Christian's life and in continuing Christ's work. The Spirit does not just offer new birth, but is a continual presence in the Christian, manifesting himself in their life and empowering them in order that they can pursue growth in holiness and be effective witnesses to God's kingdom.

We (the present authors) bring to bear an etic (outsider's) perspective on Ghanaian CMs, focusing on how the Holy Spirit's power is understood to work in the Christian's life, with regard specifically to deliverance from evil forces.⁹ What is their understanding of the Holy Spirit's role in salvation, especially sanctification? This paper explores beliefs about the Holy Spirit's sanctifying work and how Christians are expected to appropriate his power in the process of pursuing sanctification. Our primary goal is to learn from their critique of mission-founded/mainline churches, in order that we can identify aspects of our own pneumatology that are flawed or under-developed.

CM "Pneumatological Soteriology" in Context: Its Relationship with African Traditional Religion

It is worth considering the context within which this soteriology arose and developed. Both in belief and practice, CM soteriology emphasizes active, evidence-based sanctification. Asamoah-Gyadu relates this to the Ghanaian *Sunsum Sore* churches. These are sometimes referred to as "spiritual churches," or AICs, as opposed to mission-founded churches. The *Sunsum Sore* were an earlier form of AICs, a predecessor to the CMs. Asamoah-Gyadu observes that the *Sunsum Sore* form of Christianity held great appeal because it presented

---

6. Asamoah-Gyadu, "Conquering Satan," 86, emphasis ours.
7. Asamoah-Gyadu, 94.
8. Anderson and Otwang, *Tumelo*, 66, cited in Asamoah-Gyadu, *African Charismatics*, 200.
9. Merriam-Webster defines "etic" as "of, relating to, or involving analysis of cultural phenomena from the perspective of one who does not participate in the culture being studied" (Merriam-Webster, s.v. "etic," https://www.merriam-webster.com/dictionary/etic). This need not mean that one is not sympathetic to, or does not resonate with, aspects of the culture under study.

Christ as a deliverer not just from sin and damnation but also from oppression by evil spirits.[10] This Christology teaches that God's sovereign will is that Christians receive present deliverance from sickness, demonic oppression and poverty. Asamoah-Gyadu identifies in CMs a strong continuity between African Traditional Religions (ATRs) and Christianity.[11] This view of salvation is appealing because it describes the Holy Spirit as dominating the believer's life and granting them access to a life of victory, not only over sin but from all negative aspects of life in this broken world. The evidence that one is being sanctified and leading an active Christian life is that they prosper and display their dominion over evil forces.

Known for his book *Delivered from the Powers of Darkness*, Emmanuel Eni is among many West African authors who narrate vivid salvation accounts that involve dramatic battles between Satan and God.[12] Such stories often involve an individual who experiences constant temptation by Satan with "worldly" favors like promises of money and fame. Once they yield, they are captured by Satan who takes them through a series of ritualistic orientations of how the evil spirit world operates in the life of humans. At the end, through prayer, the person is delivered by the Holy Spirit and lives to warn people of involvement with demonic activity. These stories depict the two powers constantly at war.[13] The Christian's behavior reveals which power prevails in a particular situation. This is a familiar scenario not only in books but also in West African songs and films.

In describing Ghanaian Pentecostal churches, Meyer states, "They have an uncompromising attitude toward traditional religion, which they depict

---

10. Asamoah-Gyadu, *African Charismatics*, 22. Lowery has elsewhere noted "African theology's concern with identity, specifically an identity that is inculturated, liberating, full of life, and shaped by community" (Lowery, *Identity and Ecclesiology*, 46).

11. Asamoah-Gyadu, *African Charismatics*, 19. Asamoah-Gyadu argues that the African reception of the missionary enterprise was met with some dissatisfaction as it did not seem to meet the primary concerns of the Africans. He says, "They found unsatisfactory the inability of inherited Western theologies to respond to their deep-seated yearnings for protection and for the vitalizing experience of the Spirit underscored in the Bible" (19). He therefore agrees with Allan Anderson that one reason a Pentecostal/charismatic spirituality is so appealing in Africa is because it takes seriously African concerns, including an emphasis on the spirit realm (Asamoah-Gyadu, "Of 'Sour Grapes,'" 340). Another reason this form of spirituality has been so appealing is that it emphasizes experiencing the Spirit's presence and power, factors "that theologically distinguished their ecclesiology from those of historic mission denominations" (Asamoah-Gyadu, "'Go Near and Join Thyself,'" 339).

12. Eni, *Delivered from the Powers*.

13. Eni, 5. The author narrates the mysterious experiences with which he was introduced to occultism. In chapter 3 of the book, he describes his meeting with the devil that included planning to entice Christians away from spirituality through worldly lusts.

as sheerly diabolical, and constantly preach a puritan ethic as the only way to escape satanic temptations."[14] Not only do CMs shun associations with traditional religion, but also with traditional mission-founded churches. "Withdrawal from the traditional mission churches is also recommended. This is on account of their being considered too 'weak,' set in their ways and their Christianity too cerebral to provide the needed spiritual context for the nurture and sustenance of people's new religious experiences."[15] The desire, at least in part, is the commendable desire to not just speak *about* the gospel, but to see its reality *demonstrated* in lives: surely the Christ of the Gospels – present today through his Spirit – still transforms lives. With this last point, non-charismatics agree, though we differ on the details of what sorts of transformations are guaranteed to the Christian in this present life.

Accessing spiritual power through a leader is another vital aspect of the life of the CMs. The spiritual leader is charged with the responsibility of mediating this power in the affairs of their subjects. CMs place a high value on the leader's ability to employ spiritual power on behalf of their followers. A good leader must be able to intervene and disrupt the functioning of evil powers by wielding the Spirit's power. The amount of power residing in the leader is measured by their ability to offer solutions and bring harmony in the follower's life.[16] This deliverance often takes place by means of a religious leader who mediates the divine deliverance. This leader therefore is reverently referred to as "Man of God." The church looks to him as an intermediary between the spirit world and the Christian. The new believer is supposed to yield to the protection mediated by the spiritual leader, the "Big Man."[17] Converts may be taken through rituals where through the laying on of hands, the believer is revitalized, acquires more spiritual power and is freed from bondage.[18]

The process of salvation is viewed as changing covenants. Kalu notes, "A successful conversion to Christianity will require that a Christian exchange primal covenants with a new one with Jesus Christ which involves deliverance

---

14. Meyer, "'Delivered from the Powers,'" 236–55.
15. Asamoah-Gyadu, *African Charismatics*, 144.
16. Baëta, *Prophetism in Ghana*, 73–74.
17. This view of leadership seems closer to OT and ATR understandings of priesthood, where the leader holds more power and acts as a mediator. Unfortunately, there seems to be less appreciation of the priesthood of all believers as seen in the NT, which reminds Christians that each one has direct access to Christ and the Spirit's power and is also accountable for pursuing their own growth (sanctification).
18. Kalu, *African Pentecostalism*, 81.

and an alert attitude against the wiles of the enemy."[19] The Christian life is thus a constant battle between the major subjects in the covenanting experience. When the believer yields to sin, it is often interpreted that God is losing the battle, and when there is victory over sin, this is taken to mean that the devil has lost the war. The Christian is answerable to God for losing ground by sinning, and therefore will be punished through spiritual oppression and calamities. What this view does theologically is that it takes ATR views of spiritual power and inserts them into pneumatology, specifically sanctification.

This, then, is our evaluation of the CMs: there is a strong desire to make a clear and decisive break with ATRs as well as mission-founded/historic churches. However, despite this desire, ATR views have influenced aspects of the CM beliefs and practice – for instance, views of leadership, fear of the spirit world, spiritual power as being more impersonal and manipulatable by a leader and even the nature of sanctification. This last one will be our focus below.

CM Soteriology: Deliverance as a Key Aspect of Sanctification

Having briefly surveyed the context of Ghanaian CMs, we now move to focus on Asamoah-Gyadu's presentation of CM soteriology. He identifies two key emphases in CM soteriology. The first is that salvation means to come to Christ in repentance and faith being assured of forgiveness of sin, seeking him as one's personal savior. With this emphasis, Protestants agree.[20] Disagreements arise on the second emphasis, however.

The second key emphasis is that salvation "becomes a stepping-stone to being empowered by the Holy Spirit."[21] This empowerment results in a victorious Christian life. This second element is crucial because it serves to authenticate the person's claim to be a Christian. Empowerment by the Spirit is followed by producing the fruit of the Spirit, receiving spiritual gifts and experiencing "the Spirit of God arousing in them a passion for God's Kingdom."[22] Because the Spirit empowered and worked in Christ's earthly ministry, the expectation is that he continues to empower and work through Christians today, in order to demonstrate the gospel's truth.

In other words, "Pentecostal/charismatic churches draw attention to the need to bring together in ministry the Word and Spirit in order that God's

---

19. Kalu, 80.
20. Asamoah-Gyadu, "Signs, Wonders, and Ministry," 33.
21. Asamoah-Gyadu, *African Charismatics*, 135.
22. Asamoah-Gyadu, 135.

power may be evident in Christian witness."[23] From another angle, one could say that inward regeneration should lead to outward transformation, thus testifying to the truth of the gospel message. Broadly speaking, we can say that non-charismatic Protestants could agree with these two points, though unfortunately non-charismatics have sometimes tended to emphasize conversion more than transformation and empowerment by the Spirit.[24] The disagreements arise over what this transformation and empowerment should look like.

Practical Salvation

The Ghanaian charismatic movement has had its central focus on "practical salvation."[25] Asamoah-Gyadu also uses the phrase "holistic salvation" to define their view that salvation must be clearly manifested in all areas of one's life.[26] There is a linkage here between Christology (what Christ did during his earthly ministry), pneumatology (how the Spirit worked through Christ and works today through Christians), ecclesiology (how saved persons live and grow in community), and the *euangelion* (both its content and its proclamation). As Asamoah-Gyadu puts it, "When the gospel is carried in the power of the Spirit, the evidence from the life of the early church suggests that there is first 'transformation' and then 'influence'" – transformation in individual lives, then influence "because the effects of the gospel on others become palpable."[27] With these points, non-charismatics can generally agree.

However, the term "practical salvation" has a more specific meaning for CMs. It is salvation that can and will solve all kinds of problems. Such salvation brings physical healing, financial health, freedom from demonic oppression and so on. In other words, it is salvation that brings specific visible differences, leading a person toward wholeness and flourishing in this life. The mission-

---

23. Asamoah-Gyadu, "Signs, Wonders, and Ministry," 32.

24. Asamoah-Gyadu, 33. He draws upon Lesslie Newbigin's categorization of Christianity into three streams: Roman Catholicism, "orthodox" Protestantism, and Pentecostalism. We have chosen instead to say "non-charismatic Protestants" in order to avoid confusion or the implication that non-charismatic Protestants are orthodox, whereas Pentecostals are not. Non-charismatics are those Christians who put less emphasis on the *charismata*, and specifically on speaking in tongues.

25. The term "practical salvation" was derived from Lauterbach's work. She uses it to connote a salvation authenticated by domination over evil, as well as health and prosperity (Lauterbach, *History of Wealth*, 43).

26. Asamoah-Gyadu, "Signs, Wonders, and Ministry," 37.

27. Asamoah-Gyadu, 42.

founded churches emphasized "spiritual transformation" and did not appear to sufficiently address concerns like those just mentioned. This perceived lack led to the birth and rise of the *Sunsum Sore* movement.[28] "Practical salvation" must include deliverance: one who has been saved from Satan's reign *will* manifest specific evidences of that liberation. In this view, the goal is an authenticating faith, one that is qualified by consistent growth socially and economically. This differs from the classical Pentecostal view that focused on soul-searching holiness and purity of heart as a sign of deliverance.[29] CMs teach that the evidence that one is pure in heart and is growing in Christlikeness is that they can overcome social and economic obstacles together with evil spiritual hindrances.

One attraction of CMs is their claim to be relevant; Asamoah-Gyadu helpfully clarifies what is meant by this claim. According to him, "In the Ghanaian context, to speak of 'practical Christianity' or what is considered 'theologically relevant' is to speak of a God whose power is unsurpassed and who practically manifests his presence in the experiences of his people."[30] The viability of the Christian faith rests solely in the evidence of God's involvement in the normal way of life. Not only is he transforming the individual spiritually, but the individual achieves new heights in life, a realm where suffering is unexpected. A flaw in this view is that it deprives the individual of appreciating suffering as an element crucial to their sanctification. CMs clearly expect that God will always authenticate his presence to those who believe with physical evidence, namely miracles, signs and wonders, which are crucial in the believer's life.

So then, the CM perspective on salvation is broad, including spiritual freedom from Satan's rule as well as present, visible restoration to wholeness in every area of life.

> The deployment of divine resources, that is power and authority in the name and blood of Jesus – perceived in pneumatological terms as the intervention of the Holy Spirit – to provide release . . ., in order that victims may be restored to proper functioning order, that is, to health and wholeness; and being thus freed from

---

28. Baëta, *Prophetism in Ghana*, 63–64. According to Lauterbach, the "spiritual churches" – the *Sunsum Sore* – played an active role in the establishment of the CMs (*History of Wealth*, 39). Another major influence was the conventional Pentecostal movements that included Assemblies of God, the Church of Pentecost, the Apostolic Church, and the Christ Apostolic Church (*History of Wealth*, 49).

29. Fer, "Holy Spirit and the Pentecostal Habitus," 157–76.

30. Asamoah-Gyadu, *African Charismatics*, 234.

demonic influence and curses, they may enjoy God's fullness of life.³¹

Again, in CMs, "fullness of life" is clearly understood to mean flourishing and prospering in every aspect of life, both spiritual and material. Thus, in this perspective one could say that regeneration involves new inner (spiritual) life as well as external or physical changes. Though these aspects may be separated in time – inner regeneration first, then later reception of fullness of life in one's body and finances, for example – they are seen as integrally linked, even essential aspects of citizenship in God's kingdom. Thus, fullness of life in all areas is an outward manifestation of freedom from Satan's rule, hence the importance of experiencing such fullness in the present. It is not merely desirable, but imperative. While the new life is given but once, deliverance may need to occur repeatedly as the Christian falls into sin. However, this deliverance is part of salvation's application; it is a key aspect of sanctification.

In assessing CMs, Asamoah-Gyadu underscores that their theological emphasis on holistic transformation after conversion is in many ways influenced by the works of Jesus portrayed in the Gospels as well as the ATR view of salvation from all types of evil.³² The ATR concept of salvation is one of harmony with oneself and the cosmos. The person who is saved should then be protected from evil powers, and thus will flourish. The "saved" one can expect to experience deliverance from witchcraft, barrenness, sickness and other negations of life. Asamoah-Gyadu appreciates the detailed concern of CMs on holistic transformation and points out the significance of such a perspective in the context where the CMs thrive.³³ However, the lack of consistency between the extravagant expectations of "victorious life," and the reality of calamities like the COVID-19 pandemic, certainly raise significant questions about how much "fullness" a Christian can expect in this life.³⁴

As Asamoah-Gyadu describes it,

---

31. Asamoah-Gyadu, "Conquering Satan," 94.
32. Asamoah-Gyadu, *African Charismatics*, 49.
33. Asamoah-Gyadu, 137.
34. Asamoah-Gyadu's article "Pentecostalism and Coronavirus: Reframing the Message of Health-and-Wealth in a Pandemic Era" explores various responses by Pentecostal preachers to the pandemic, which directly challenged their "triumphalist assumptions on faith and evil in human life" (162). He notes responses such as a return to eschatological themes, or prophecies, before concluding "Many of the principles of prosperity come unstuck in the face of misfortune, calamity, and evil, and the hope is that the coronavirus has among other things exposed the areas of deficiency" (172).

> In the Christianity of the CMs, salvation is seen as something to be *experienced*. Their key "soteriological goals" in this life therefore include the realization of "transformation and empowerment," "healing and deliverance," and "prosperity and success" in the lives of believers. In an experiential movement, the emphasis on "personality transformation" underlying the spirituality of the CMs is evident in these soteriological goals.[35]

From a non-charismatic Protestant perspective, we agree that salvation, specifically sanctification, includes transformation and empowerment by the Spirit, but the details of what that empowerment would look like may differ, and with regards to healing and prosperity, we would say that these can be given by God but are not *guaranteed* in this life.

Just as many non-charismatic views of regeneration, CMs emphasize the importance of conversion in the Christian life. The individual must choose to repent and turn to Christ in order to become a child of God. However, conversion is only part of the process of regeneration through the Holy Spirit. In CM views, "salvation in the African context involves not just repentance through the confession of personal sins but also the renunciation of intended and unintended participation in 'demonic' cultural practices, such as 'rites of passage', and the repudiation of the effects of generational sins and curses upon a person's life."[36] One must convert, then proceed to repudiate one's evil past, and this repudiation may need to occur repeatedly. The practice of repudiation may lead some to counter, doesn't regeneration by its very nature mean a break with generational sins and curses? Must a believer always seek a separate and subsequent deliverance from these? In the CM view, the answer is yes, one must renounce such things and seek deliverance.

In the CM view, one reason Christians need deliverance is because committing a sin leads the Christian back into "captivity to supernatural evil," and this captivity is revealed in issues such as substance addictions, "negative" emotions (such as anger), unfaithfulness to one's partner, poverty and so on. An individual may also be facing spiritual oppression because of the name they were given at birth, and thus that person ought to choose a new, "Christian" name.[37] People struggling with these issues are interpreted as being oppressed by Satanic powers, and thus they need to ask the Spirit to deliver them.[38] They

---

35. Asamoah-Gyadu, *African Charismatics*, 133.
36. Asamoah-Gyadu, "Mission to 'Set the Captives Free,'" 391.
37. Asamoah-Gyadu, "Of 'Sour Grapes,'" 343–44.
38. Asamoah-Gyadu, "Mission to 'Set the Captives Free,'" 395.

are expected to renounce sinful emotions and behaviors, in seeking this divine, Spirit-given deliverance.

Some aspects of this view are helpful: it reminds the Christian that they have a role to play in sanctification, emphasizing their agency. The emphasis on personal experience means "religion is expected to be a matter of personal choice rather than of institutional presence."[39] This view of salvation is one we agree with, and the emphasis on a strong personal commitment indicates an area that non-charismatics need to re-emphasize, to fight against nominal Christianity. As Asamoah-Gyadu notes, in seeking out deliverance, the CMs "urge people to break decisively with the past, take their destinies into their own hands, and make personal choices regarding how they relate to the God of Christian salvation."[40] The fact that CMs feel a need to emphasize this area does indicate that at least in perception, mainline Protestant churches have fallen short in this area and need to re-consider their approach. Western missionaries have sometimes been justly accused of focusing so much on conversion that ecclesiology and sanctification are secondary at best. In pragmatic terms, there is nothing wrong with evangelism crusades, but intentional discipleship on the ongoing work of the Spirit in a Christian's life and his empowering to pursue sanctification has been insufficient ("sanctification" meaning growth in Christlikeness in character, not necessarily the "practical salvation" or "deliverance" sense used by CMs).

Does this deliverance teaching imply that God will not set a person free unless they first request it? Asamoah-Gyadu concludes that Pentecostals hold the view that a regenerated person may still be under the power of an ancestral curse, for instance, if the individual has not renounced all previous ties.[41] In this case, it is up to the individual to make a decisive break with their past and take the step of seeking deliverance. Certainly, one hopes that the oppressed or struggling person desires such transformation, but it is helpful also to note that there are times in Scripture where God freed people who had not requested deliverance. One thinks of the female slave who was not herself requesting deliverance from her demonic possession, from whom Paul cast out the unclean spirit (Acts 16:16–18).

Asamoah-Gyadu suggests another danger. If the demonic element is over-emphasized, it actually eclipses the role of humanity by suggesting that humans

---

39. Asamoah-Gyadu, "Encountering Jesus," 376, citing B. Wilson, *The Functions of Religion*, 199.
40. Asamoah-Gyadu, "Of 'Sour Grapes,'" 336–37.
41. Asamoah-Gyadu, 343.

are helpless (and thus not responsible agents) in regard to demonic activity. If there is an "'uncompromising link' between misfortune and mystical agents, it creates the danger of diminished individual and corporate responsibility that the Bible" upholds.[42] He gives the examples of Ananias and Sapphira, as well as Judas, all of whose actions were instigated by Satan, but whom their fellow Christians held responsible for their actions.[43] Asamoah-Gyadu rightly concludes that even if temptation seems irresistible, "it does not diminish personal responsibility."[44] We strongly concur with Asamoah-Gyadu's view that while demonic activity is presented in the Bible as real and powerful, it is *never* presented as negating or removing the individual or community's responsibility in how they respond.

Note the paradox of the CM position here. The believer is urged to make a personal commitment to Christ and to seek out deliverance when needed, both steps that indicate a person has and must exercise their agency. At the same time, the emphasis on deliverance can be so strong that it ends up diminishing the individual's agency and responsibility, leaving the Christian almost at the whim of the demonic realm.

Another way of understanding the Holy Spirit's deliverance among CMs is to describe the Pentecostal/charismatic view as presenting "'an interventionist theology' which is embraced. Asante [culture] says, 'The African reality demands a savior who has the power not only to deliver the believer from evil powers but also transform the lives of the bewitched and the dehumanized.'"[45] What can be seen here is that the Spirit's power brings new life, but also calls the converted person to exercise that same power, asking the Spirit for deliverance from past sinful ties. If the emphasis is on reliance upon the Spirit's power for growth, then it makes sense why the CM view of deliverance is linked to sanctification rather than regeneration. The Christian is expected to live a different life than that of a non-believer, but can only do so through continued reliance on the Holy Spirit and his divine power, a vital reminder that the Christian life cannot be lived in one's own strength. Without the Spirit's power, a Christian will surely succumb to demonic influence.

The emphasis on the ongoing activity of demonic spirits raises a question (not unique to the CM context) about regeneration and the world of the evil spirits, precisely what does it mean to say that regeneration by the Holy Spirit

---

42. Asamoah-Gyadu, *African Charismatics*, 197.
43. Asamoah-Gyadu, 179, 197.
44. Asamoah-Gyadu, 197.
45. Asamoah-Gyadu, "Mission to 'Set the Captives Free,'" 391.

makes one a new creation and sets one free from Satan's reign? Does it mean that any previous curses are broken when one is made new? Can one who has been born from above by the Spirit still suffer from demonic possession (as distinguished from demonic oppression)?[46] There appears to be no doubt among CMs that the Holy Spirit's power is greater than that of the demonic hordes and that he is indeed capable of delivering a person from demonic activity; the discussion revolves more around how vulnerable is a Christian to demonic influence, and what one must do to be delivered. Unfortunately, there is also a crucial error in the CM perspective; that in every case present deliverance – never suffering – is God's will for the Christian.[47] We use the term "crucial" here deliberately – it is a foundational matter to miss that suffering is part of discipleship. It is also crucial in the sense of misunderstanding the cross itself, as Jesus calls his disciples to take up their crosses and follow him; this call seems to be missed by CMs.

Furthermore, the CM expectations of deliverance resurface debates on how anticipation of transformation in a believer's life links with eschatology and God's kingdom. CMs expect to see a great deal of the kingdom in the present – not just changed hearts and actions, but also material changes in health and financial status.[48] From these writers' view, that indicates an over-realized eschatology that leaves little room for the "not yet" of the kingdom. Asamoah-Gyadu agrees, observing that, "This [Pentecostal/charismatic] theology of dominion which broadens the notion of transformation to encompass both spiritual and material changes in everyday life means that eschatological issues may lie a little subdued in neo-Pentecostal preaching."[49] The emphasis is less on Christ's return and more on present-day prospering.[50] This is not to say that eschatology has disappeared, but that it has significantly diminished in importance, as total "fullness of life" is expected now. "The CMs anticipate the 'return of Christ,' but this theme does not feature too prominently in their teachings."[51] If Christ's second advent is diminished, then one wonders what

---

46. According to Asamoah-Gyadu, "Exponents of 'healing and deliverance' generally make a distinction between 'demonic possession' and 'demonic oppression' in relation to the activities of evil powers" ("Mission to 'Set the Captives Free,'" 395).

47. Asamoah-Gyadu, "Encountering Jesus," 376.

48. Unfortunately, one major component of the CMs is the prosperity gospel. For instance, see Asamoah-Gyadu, "Did Jesus Wear Designer Robes," and "'Your Miracle Is on the Way,'" 5–26.

49. Asamoah-Gyadu, "Your Body Is a Temple," 5.

50. Asamoah-Gyadu, "In Search of a Better Country," 160.

51. Asamoah-Gyadu, *African Charismatics*, 152–53.

specifically CMs hope for when Christ returns. If believers' lives can be freed from the effects of sin and Satan in the present, and "fullness of life" (in terms of health, wealth and deliverance from hardships) can be expected in the present, why should one long for the future return of Christ, and indeed what will be changed upon his return? What aspects of sanctification remain to be fulfilled in the future? These are indeed questions that are not just theoretical and abstract, but that impact daily living and one's view of the world.

Putting aside eschatological issues, we affirm that CMs view the Christian life as a battle against evil, and in this battle one must consciously call upon the Holy Spirit to prevail over demonic forces. Their non-charismatic brethren would interpret this battle against satanic forces as one aspect of sanctification. Once we align ourselves with Christ, we can expect to be "hated" by the "world," in Johannine language, and thus the Christian life always includes spiritual warfare. However, the CMs tend to teach that upon seeking the Spirit's power, the Christian will necessarily be delivered from attack and hardships, which unfortunately leaves little or no space for sanctification *through* hardships; as Asamoah-Gyadu notes, their theodicy is woefully lacking.[52] In a sense, one can say that their focus on deliverance seems no longer to be linked to a desire for sanctification as non-charismatic Christians understand it (progressive growth in holiness and Christlikeness), but rather a firm belief that is God's will for Christians to always live a prosperous life in the here and now.[53] Or, to rephrase this, the CMs could say that a prosperous life in the present is an indication of holiness, and on this we disagree. This error serves as a grievous and timely warning to every Christian. One may come to misidentify their desire for immediate deliverance as identical with God's sovereign will in every circumstance. In other words, instead of the overemphasis on the future and eternal, of which missionaries were sometimes accused, there is now an overemphasis on the physical and temporal to the neglect of the eternal.[54]

Despite this significant error, Asamoah-Gyadu concludes that "The bottom line . . . is that in the CMs salvation is expected to be a decisive transition resulting in personal transformation, that is, a new life with a new lifestyle," and "salvation involves God's response to human sin as well as the way in which the saved relate to the world."[55] In part, the CMs are reacting to nominal Christianity, in which a person attends church but does not display a changed

---

52. Asamoah-Gyadu, 189.
53. Asamoah-Gyadu, "In Search of a Better Country," 160.
54. Our thanks to Joshua Barron for clarifying our thinking on this point.
55. Asamoah-Gyadu, *African Charismatics*, 138.

lifestyle. The CM movement is right to stress that salvation must include a change in the lifestyle of the person who truly follows Christ. They are also right to criticize churches that so stress conversion that discipleship and expectation of transformation are downplayed.

Conclusions

From our own perspective, much of what the CMs believe about deliverance must be rejected, such as their notion that deliverance necessarily means absence of suffering in this life. However, their emphasis upon seeking deliverance by the Holy Spirit as a key aspect of sanctification challenges our own theological tendency to emphasize inner spiritual change, too often at the expense of neglecting transformation of one's lifestyle. It also challenges a tendency to focus upon the Spirit as the giver of new life, so much so that his ongoing role in sanctification is minimized or ignored. In other words, the CMs point out to us that while they have excesses and errors, we too have deficiencies in our pneumatology, particularly in the area of sanctification.

While CMs can be criticized, the overarching goal in this paper is for non-charismatics to learn positive lessons from this movement. The CMs desire to stand as a clear contrast to nominal, anemic forms of Christianity. They are not for the faint of heart; they require a Christian to take a clear stand and wrestle with God to procure blessings. They expect to see God through the Spirit at work in the world. What are some of the positive lessons non-charismatics can learn from the CMs? We will highlight two of the lessons we believe are important for pneumatology among non-CMs.

First, Asamoah-Gyadu highlights that the emphasis on renouncing evil influences compels a believer to take responsibility of their own actions and spiritual life. This we affirm and acknowledge needs to be better taught and modeled in non-charismatic churches. Related to this, the ongoing role of the Holy Spirit in sanctification is emphasized, which reminds Christians that the Spirit has a vital role to play, one that does not end with regeneration. The CMs remind us that the regenerate person should seek to live life empowered by the Spirit, expecting to see their choices, desires and habits transformed by that very same Spirit who empowers Christians to witness and to grow in experiential holiness. Christians need to take responsibility for their choices and for their spiritual growth; if they do not, we will not have a deep, strong Christianity that can withstand the storms of sinful human and demonic forces.

Second, one CM critique of traditional, Western mission-founded churches is that their form of Christianity is "considered too 'weak,' set in their ways and their Christianity too cerebral."[56] The way in which Christ is proclaimed seems incomplete, and lives that should reflect the gospel are not as compelling as they ought to be; gospel proclamation and demonstration are felt to be lacking. This is a clarion call for non-charismatic Protestants to reflect more carefully on the gospel. Here we agree with Asamoah-Gyadu, who concludes that "despite any reservations one may have about how some of Africa's independent churches have operated, we cannot fault them for insisting that [sic] the cerebral nature of historic mission Christianity and their moral permissiveness were at variance with biblical teaching."[57] Before we critique the theology or praxis of the CMs, we must take stock of our own theology and praxis. We have not always preached or practiced a holistic gospel, but sometimes a purely spiritualized, internalized one that does not reflect what we see in the NT and in Jesus specifically.[58] And our lives have not lived up to what we preach, and thus we must confess our own hypocrisy, which has further damaged the cause of the gospel.

It is time, we might say, to work at taking the plank out of our own eyes before we attempt to remove the speck of sawdust in the eyes of our brethren (Luke 6:41–42). This does not downplay our concerns and critiques of the CMs, but reminds us that we must begin with reforming ourselves; we must take responsibility for our own failings and shortcomings. In truth, though it is painful, we must accept and be humbled by the rebuke of the CMs. Positively, we strongly affirm that following Christ is meant to transform heart, mind and actions; the gospel should be good news for the suffering and outcast of society. Where churches have failed to grasp this, they have failed to properly proclaim the gospel as good news that addresses all aspects of the Christian's life.

More could be said about the CMs, and more lessons learned from them, but for now we content ourselves with these two lessons that can help non-charismatics to reevaluate our own grasp on the gospel, our expectations (or lack of) regarding transformation and empowerment to proclaim the gospel in word and deed and our need to take responsibility for pursuing growth in the Christian life through the Spirit's power.

---

56. Asamoah-Gyadu, 144.

57. Asamoah-Gyadu, "'Go Near and Join Thyself,'" 342.

58. We do not agree with the connotations of "practical salvation," but we do concur that the gospel is intended to impact lives in more than just internal ways and that we can and should expect to see the Spirit at work today as the gospel is proclaimed and lived out. The gospel *is* holistic!

Bibliography

Anderson, Allan H. "Contextualization in Pentecostalism: A Multicultural Perspective." *International Bulletin of Mission Research* 41, no. 1 (2017): 29–40.

Anderson, Allan H., and Samuel Otwang. *Tumelo: The Faith of African Pentecostals in South Africa*. Pretoria: University of South Africa, 1993.

Anderson, George, Jr. "Ghana's Neo-Prophetic Pentecostal/Charismatic Christianity: Future Prospects." *ERATS Journal of Theological and Religious Studies* 5, no. 1 (2019): 16–27.

Asamoah-Gyadu, J. Kwabena. *African Charismatics: Current Developments within Independent Indigenous Pentecostalism in Ghana*. Boston: Brill, 2005.

———. "'Broken Calabashes and Covenants of Fruitfulness': Cursing Barrenness in Contemporary African Christianity." *Journal of Religion in Africa* 37, no. 4 (2007): 437–60.

———. "Conquering Satan, Demons, Principalities, and Powers: Ghanaian Traditional and Christian Perspectives on Religion, Evil, and Deliverance." In *Coping with Evil in Religion and Culture: Case Studies*, edited by Nelly van Doorn-Harder and Lourens Minnema, 85–103. Current of Encounter 35. Amsterdam: Editions Rodofi; Leiden: Brill, 2008.

———. "Did Jesus Wear Designer Robes?" *Lausanne Movement*, Lausanne Content Library, 1 November 2009. https://www.lausanne.org/content/did-jesus-wear-designer-robes.

———. "Encountering Jesus in African Christianity: A Ghanaian Evangelical/Pentecostal Thought on Faith, Experience, and Hope in Christ." *HTS Theological Studies* 62, no. 2 (2006): 363–77.

———. "'Go Near and Join Thyself to This Chariot . . .': African Pneumatic Movements and Transformational Discipleship." *International Review of Mission* 106, no. 2 (2017): 336–55.

———. "In Search of a Better Country: Migration and Prosperity Hermeneutics in Contemporary African Pentecostalism." *PentecoStudies* 17, no. 2 (2018): 158–79.

———. "Mission to 'Set the Captives Free': Healing, Deliverance, and Generational Curses in Ghanaian Pentecostalism." *International Review of Mission* 93, no. 370–371 (July/October 2004): 389–406.

———. "Of 'Sour Grapes' and 'Children's Teeth': Inherited Guilt, Human Rights and Processes of Restoration in Ghanaian Pentecostalism." *Exchange* 33, no. 4 (2004): 334–53.

———. "Pentecostalism and Coronavirus: Reframing the Message of Health-and-Wealth in a Pandemic Era." *Spiritus* 6, no. 1 (2021): 157–74.

———. "Signs, Wonders, and Ministry: The Gospel in the Power of the Spirit." *Evangelical Review of Theology* 33, no. 1 (2009): 32–46.

———. "'Your Body Is a Temple': Conversion Narratives in African-Led Eastern European Pentecostalism." *Pastoral Psychology* 58, no. 1 (2009): 1–14.

———. "'Your Miracle Is on the Way': Oral Roberts and Mediated Pentecostalism in Africa." *Spiritus* 3, no. 1 (2018): 5–26.

Baëta, C.G . *Prophetism in Ghana: A Study of Some "Spiritual" Churches*. London: SCM Press, 1962.

Beckmann, David M. *Eden Revival: Spiritual Churches in Ghana*. St. Louis: Concordia, 1975.

Eni, Emmanuel. *Delivered from the Powers of Darkness*. Lagos, Nigeria: Scripture Union, 1988.

Fer, Yannick. "The Holy Spirit and the Pentecostal Habitus: Elements for a Sociology of Institution in Classical Pentecostalism." *Nordic Journal of Religion and Society* 23, no. 2 (2010): 157–76.

Kalu, Ogbu. *African Pentecostalism: An Introduction*. New York: Oxford University Press, 2008.

Lauterbach, Karen. *A History of Wealth, Power, and Religion in Asante*. Copenhagen, Denmark: Palgrave Macmillan, 2017.

Lowery, Stephanie A. *Identity and Ecclesiology: Their Relationship among Select African Theologians*. Eugene: Pickwick, 2017.

Meyer, Birgit. "'Delivered from the Powers of Darkness': Confessions of Satanic Riches in Christian Ghana." *Africa: Journal of the International Africa Institute* 65, no. 2 (1995): 236–55.

List of Contributors

Kwaku Boamah is a lecturer at the Department for the Study of Religions, University of Ghana, Legon. As an ordained minister of the Methodist Church Ghana (MGC), he is currently serving as a Campus Ministry Coordinator of the Northern Accra Diocese of the MCG and Chapel Warden of the Akuafo Hall of the University of Ghana. He holds a PhD in Religions with a speciality in Early Church history from the University of Ghana and MA in Religious Roots of Europe from the Aarhus University, Denmark.

Heleen Joziasse is a feminist theologian and an ordained minister in the Protestant Church in The Netherlands. Between 2009–2014 she served as lecturer in the Faculty of Theology at St. Paul's University, Limuru, Kenya. In 2020 she obtained a PhD from Utrecht University, The Netherlands, with research entitled "Women's Faith Seeking Life: Lived Christologies and the Transformation of Gender Relations in Two Kenyan Churches."

John Michael Kiboi is an ordained priest in the Anglican Church of Kenya, serving as a Senior Lecturer in the Faculty of Theology at St. Paul's University, Limuru, Kenya. He holds a PhD in Dogmatic Theology from the Catholic University of Eastern Africa, Kenya. Previously he served as a parish priest in the diocese of Bungoma and Principal at Wycliffe Centre for Theology, Canada. Currently, he is the leader of PhD programs in the Faculty of Theology at St. Paul's University, Kenya.

Jeffrey S. Krohn has served in the arena of theological education for more than twenty years. Originally from the United States, he is currently Professor of Biblical Studies at Evangelical Theological College in Addis Ababa, Ethiopia. Previously, he ministered in rural and urban settings in the country of Peru. He holds a PhD in Biblical Studies/Hermeneutics from London School of Theology/Middlesex University, UK.

Stephanie A. Lowery is a lecturer in theology and coordinator of the BTh and DTh programs at Africa International University, Kenya, and also teaches at Kalamba School of Leadership as well as serving part-time in the Kalamba church district. She grew up in Kenya and considers Ukambani home. Her research interests include African theologies, African ecclesiological models, missional theology and hermeneutics and the Trinity.

Kenosi Molato works as a researcher at SHINE Africa Project and as a national director of Romans Project in Botswana, a position he has held since 2014. He is currently a PhD candidate in Systematic Theology at South African Theological Seminary.

Esther Mombo is a Professor at St. Paul's University, Limuru, Kenya, Faculty of Theology. She has served as Academic Dean for seven years and Deputy Vice Chancellor Academic Affairs for six years and as the Director International Partnership and Alumni relations for seven years. Currently she is the East Africa regional coordinator of the Circle of Concerned Women Theologians in Africa. She holds a PhD from Edinburgh University, UK, in African Church History.

David K. Ngaruiya is an Associate Professor, former acting Deputy Vice Chancellor for Academic Affairs and Director of the PhD in Theological Studies program at International Leadership University, Kenya. He holds a PhD in Intercultural Studies from Trinity Evangelical Divinity School, USA. He served as chair of the Africa Society of Evangelical Theology (2015–2016). He has published journal and book articles and served as co-editor and contributor to *Communities of Faith in Africa and African Diaspora* (Pickwick Publications, 2013) and was a director of the research study that produced *African Christian Leadership* (Langham Global Library, 2019).

Moses Iliya Ogidis is a minister with Evangelical Church Winning All (ECWA) in Nigeria. Currently he is a PhD in Theology (New Testament) candidate at St. Paul's University, Limuru, Kenya.

Jacob Kwame Opata is a graduate student at Trinity Theological Seminary, Ghana pursuing Systematic Studies. He holds a Master of Arts in Ministry from Trinity Theological Seminary and is an associate pastor with the International Central Gospel Church.

Rodney L. Reed is a missionary educator who has been serving at Africa Nazarene University in Nairobi, Kenya, since 2001. Currently, he is the Deputy Vice-Chancellor of Academic Affairs, a position he has held since 2010. Prior to that, he served as the Chair of the Department of Religion for nine years. He holds a PhD in Theological Ethics from Drew University, USA, and is an ordained minister in the Church of the Nazarene.

Danson Ottawa Wafula is a podcast host at The Christian Life Podcast and serves as a pastoral intern at Hope City Bible Church in Nairobi. He currently works at the Association of Evangelicals in Africa (AEA) in the communications and programs department. He holds a Bachelor of Theology degree from Africa International University, Kenya, and is currently enrolled in the same institution pursuing a Master of Divinity in Biblical Studies. Danson has a passion for theological scholarship, the church and apologetics.

Subject and Author Index

A
African Traditional Religion 113
African women's theologies 92
AICs 26, 28, 94
AINC 96
Anderson, Allan 112
Anim, Peter 26, 29
Anomoean 51
Asamoah-Gyadu, J. Kwabena 126, 128
Augustine 33, 35, 46
Azusa experience 19
Azusa Street Revival 24

B
Beerden, K. 5
Born, Jacob 106
Bwire, John Peter 10

C
charismata 19, 23, 26
   cessation, theory of 20
charismatic 18, 136, 138
Christianity
   African 45
   practical 132
church
   African 45
   Nigerian 9-15
churches
   African Independant 106
   African Pentecostal 106
   evangelical 3, 9
   fire 116
Confessions 34
Congar, Yves 80
conservatives, Christian 57
Creed 34, 37, 47, 93, 117

D
day of Pentecost 6, 11
De Genesi ad litteram 34–35
deliverance 128
De Trinitate 41, 43
Dionysius of Halicarnassus 5
diversity 13

E
Eni, Emmanuel 128
ethics, Christian 84
exaltation of Christ 79

F
female disciples 4, 8
Ferguson, Sinclair B. 74, 80
finger of God 44
Frame, John 81
functional theologians 61

G
gender 93
Gerber, Chad 33
Grayson, James H. 23

H
Harris, Grace 113
Harris, William Wadé 26, 29
heresies 67
   pneumatological 51
heresy 47
hermeneutics, African 46
Hermon Church 108–9
Herrick, Greg 60
Hinga, Teresia 100
Holy Spirit 36–37, 39, 109–10
   biblical motifs of 116
   book of 2
   deity of 117

fruit of 118
gifts of 118
person of 110
personhood of 73
possessed by/with 115
power of 109
name of 75
work of 74, 107
honor/shame worldviews 122

I
inclusivity 2, 15
interpretation, Eurocentric 10

J
Jehovah's Witnesses 73

K
Kalu, Ogbu 113
Kealotswe, Obed N. O. 110
Kenya, neo-Pentecostalism in 53
kerygmatic 4
Kivuli, John 96

L
leadership 95, 98
Leupp, Roderick T. 77
Lewis, C. S. 86
love of God 39

M
MacRobert, Iain 112
mainline churches 19
Maluleke, Tinyiko 112
martyrdoms 23
martyrs 44
Migliore, Daniel 57
ministries, charismatic 126
missio ad intra 59
mission 67
modalism 119
modalistic monarchianism 58
modus operandi 18
Montanism 23
Montanus 22

Monyai, Keikanetswe 109
movements, neo-Pentecostal 27
mutuality, Christian 13

N
neo-Pentecostal 28, 50
neo-Pentecostalism 53
Ngong, David, Tonghou 80
Nigeria, culture of 10
Nyabwari, Bernard Gechiko 54

O
Oduyoye, Mercy A. 2
Omenyo, Cephas N. 19, 26
ontological-existential 62

P
Paraclete 75–76, 93
parousia 4, 24
Pentecost 4, 20, 81
Pentecostal 130
Pentacostalism
    African 113
    black 112
people with disabilities 5
Persecution 6
person with disabilities 5
Plotinian thinking 33
pneumatology 51, 53, 72, 96, 98
    African 92
    African women's 98
    Augustinian 44
    functional 63
    Trinitarian 63
Pneumatomachians 51
postcolonial 102
Postmodernity 55
practical salvation 131

Q
quadriga 40, 46

S
salvation 130, 132
sanctification 83, 134–35

Seventh-day Adventists 54
Seymour, William J. 24
Sindima, Harvey J. 9
skeptic 56
Slee, Nicole 93
speaking in tongues 108, 116, 120
Spirit 20, 23
spirit possession 113, 119
spiritual experiences 107
spiritual sickness 108, 121
Stott, John R. W. 2, 4
Sumsum Sore 25
syncretism 95

T
Tertullian 22–23
Tertullianistae 22
theological misinterpretation 10
theologians, African 45
theology
    African 94
    African women's 92
    Reformed 62
Thiselton, Anthony C. 55
Tonghou Ngong, David 80
Trevett, Christine 21, 24
Trinity 36
tritheism 58

V
vinculum caritas 38

W
Waggoner, J. H. 54
Williams, David J. 3
Williams, Norman 41

Y
young people 15
    New Testament 7

Scripture Index

OLD TESTAMENT

Genesis
1:1 83
1:2 .... 75, 117
3:8 75
4:7 73

Exodus
3:13–15 74
3:14–15 78
3:15 76
6:3 76
6:7 76
14:21 75
15:3 76
15:8 75
23:21 76
33:19 76
34:5–7 76

Leviticus
24:11 76

Deuteronomy
6:4 37
28:58 76

1 Samuel
16 118
19 118

Job
33:4 83

Ecclesiastes
1:9–10 18
4:9 xiii

Psalms
25:10 84
30:4 76
31:5 84
33:6 83
57:10 84
83:18 76
86:15 84
89:14 84
96:2 76
97:12 76
104:30 .... 73, 83
119:160 83
135:13 76
145:21 76

Isaiah
11:2–3 117
42:8 .... 73–74, 76
44:24 83

Jeremiah
16:21 76
33:2 76

Ezekiel
36:21–23 76

Hosea
12:5 76

Joel
2:28–29 .... 7, 12

Amos
3:7 86–87
4:13 52

Zechariah
1:9 52

NEW TESTAMENT

Matthew
1:21 .... 74, 76, 78
1:25 .... 74, 76
12:28 44
12:32 117
14:15–21 7
28:18–20 79

28:19 76–78

Mark
6:53–44 7
10:13–16 6
13:19 83
14:36 78

Luke
1:26–38 5
1:31 73
2:21 76
3:22 74
5:12–26 5
6:41–42 140

7:35 73	2:1 11–12	**Romans**
9:10–17 6	2:1–42 7	1:4 83
9:12–17 7	2:1–47 .... xii, 1, 12, 14–15	3:24 83
11:20 44	2:3 74	3:26 83
14:23 37	2:8–11 7	5:14 73
22:12 11	2:17–18 95	5:21 73
23:55–56 12	2:32 83	8:4 83
24:47 76	2:33 .... 75, 81	8:9 80
24:48 79	2:38–39 20	8:11 83
24:49 74	2:41 6	8:15 78
	2:42 .... 8, 13–14	8:29 .... 78, 83, 85, 118
John	2:47 6	11:36 37
1:1 78	4:4 6	15:16 83
1:3 83	4:12 76	16:1–16 14
1:10 83	4:29 8	
1:12 76	4:31 73	**1 Corinthians**
1:14 .... 78, 84	4:32–37 8	1:2 83
2:19–21 78	5:14 7	1:10 76
3:5–6 83	5:15–16 8	1:30 83
3:8 74	5:40–41 8	6:11 .... 76, 83, 85, 118
4:24 67	6:3 73	8:6 83
5:43 76	6:7 6	11:5 11
6:5–15 7	8:1–40 7	12:1 118
6:63 83	8:1 6	12:1–11 .... 65, 67
7:37–39 74	8:12 8	12:1–31 20
10:10 96	9 .... 4, 8	12:4 44
10:17–18 83	9:32–43 8	12:7–11 95
14:15–17 .... 2, 12	10 7	13:1–3 118
14:16 .... 60, 75–76, 117	10:9–23 7	14 118–20
14:17 .... 81, 84	11:19–21 7	15:15 83
14:26 .... 75, 80–81	11:24 73	15:45 80
15:26 .... 53, 75, 79, 84–85	12:12 8	
16:8–11 118	13:43–47 8	**2 Corinthians**
16:13 84	13:52 73	1:22 74
16:14 79	15:9 83	3:6 83
17:11–12 76	15:26 76	3:18 .... 74, 83
20:31 76	16:7 80	4:6 83
	16:11–15 8	5:18–19 83
Acts	16:16–18 135	6:6 73
1:1–2 4	17:31 83	13:14 76
1:4 75	18:24 8	
1:8 .... 2, 79	18:26 8	**Galatians**
1:12–14 4	28:14 15	4:6 80
1:14–15 12		4:16 78
1:15 11		5:22–23 118

Ephesians
1:3–4	83
1:7	83
1:13	74
1:14	74
2:4–5	83
2:8	83
2:13–16	14
4:15–16	83
4:21	84
4:30	74
5:25–27	83

Philippians
1:19	80

Colossians
1:15	66, 78
1:16	83
1:18	78

1 Thessalonians
1:5	73
1:10	83

2 Thessalonians
2:13	83

1 Timothy
2:12	11
3:16	83

2 Timothy
1:6–7	20

Titus
2:14	83
3:5	83
3:6	83

Hebrews
1:14	52
2:11	83
9:14	75, 78
10:10	83
10:29	75
12:14	85

1 Peter
1:3	83
1:11	80
4:14	75
3:18	83

2 Peter
1:8–9	119
1:21	73

1 John
2:1	76, 78
2:2	83
2:27	75
4:6	75, 78
5:6	84
5:7–8	73
5:10	84

Revelation
Revelation	42
1:4	74
3:1	74
3:7	84
4:5	74
5:6	74
11:11	75
19:10	75
19:11	84

Langham Literature and its imprints are a ministry of Langham Partnership.

Langham Partnership is a global fellowship working in pursuit of the vision God entrusted to its founder John Stott –

> *to facilitate the growth of the church in maturity and Christ-likeness through raising the standards of biblical preaching and teaching.*

Our vision is to see churches in the Majority World equipped for mission and growing to maturity in Christ through the ministry of pastors and leaders who believe, teach and live by the word of God.

Our mission is to strengthen the ministry of the word of God through:
- nurturing national movements for biblical preaching
- fostering the creation and distribution of evangelical literature
- enhancing evangelical theological education

especially in countries where churches are under-resourced.

Our ministry

Langham Preaching partners with national leaders to nurture indigenous biblical preaching movements for pastors and lay preachers all around the world. With the support of a team of trainers from many countries, a multi-level programme of seminars provides practical training, and is followed by a programme for training local facilitators. Local preachers' groups and national and regional networks ensure continuity and ongoing development, seeking to build vigorous movements committed to Bible exposition.

Langham Literature provides Majority World preachers, scholars and seminary libraries with evangelical books and electronic resources through publishing and distribution, grants and discounts. The programme also fosters the creation of indigenous evangelical books in many languages, through writer's grants, strengthening local evangelical publishing houses, and investment in major regional literature projects, such as one volume Bible commentaries like *The Africa Bible Commentary* and *The South Asia Bible Commentary*.

Langham Scholars provides financial support for evangelical doctoral students from the Majority World so that, when they return home, they may train pastors and other Christian leaders with sound, biblical and theological teaching. This programme equips those who equip others. Langham Scholars also works in partnership with Majority World seminaries in strengthening evangelical theological education. A growing number of Langham Scholars study in high quality doctoral programmes in the Majority World itself. As well as teaching the next generation of pastors, graduated Langham Scholars exercise significant influence through their writing and leadership.

To learn more about Langham Partnership and the work we do visit **langham.org**

www.ingramcontent.com/pod-product-compliance
Lightning Source LLC
Chambersburg PA
CBHW070539170426
43200CB00011B/2482